Optimize Quality for Business Outcomes

A Practical Approach to Software Testing

Andreas Golze

Mark Sarbiewski

Alain Zahm

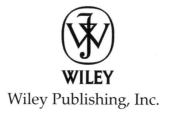

WILEY

Wiley Publishing, Inc.

Published by

Wiley Publishing, Inc.
111 River Street
Hoboken, NJ 07030-5774

www.wiley.com

Copyright ©2008 by Wiley Publishing, Inc., Indianapolis, Indiana

Published by Wiley Publishing, Inc., Indianapolis, Indiana

Published simultaneously in Canada

For general information on our other products and services, please contact our Customer Care Department within the U.S. at 800-762-2974, outside the U.S. at 317-572-3993, or fax 317-572-4002.

For technical support, please visit www.wiley.com/techsupport.

Wiley also publishes its books in a variety of electronic formats. Some content that appears in print may not be available in electronic books.

Library of Congress Control Number: 2008928205

ISBN: 978-0-470-404669

Manufactured in the United States of America

10 9 8 7 6 5 4 3 2 1

Contents

Chapter 2 Testing the Business Requirements: Start at the Root of the Problem 29

Chapter 3 Test Rules: Build the Backbone for Effective Testing 41

Chapter 4 Test Cases: Let's Get Down to the Real Stuff. 61

Chapter 5 Test Optimization: Balancing Risk and Effort 83

Chapter 6   Why Bother with Non-Functional Testing? 113

Chapter 7   Application Security Testing: The Next Frontier 149

Chapter 8   Test Sourcing: How Outsourcing Improves Cost Effective Testing. **179**

Chapter 9   *SUCCESSFUL* Goal-Driven KPI Approach . . **191**

Acknowledgements

This book would not have been possible without the help of many fine people. We'd like to thank those who have contributed ideas and those who have shaped our thoughts and concepts over the years.

First, we'd like to offer a special acknowledgement and thanks to Charlie Li and Shel Prince, who were co-authors in the first two editions. Their contribution and efforts laid the foundation for this book.

In addition, we've received help and encouragement from many departments within HP, as well as from many friends and colleagues outside the company. HP organizations lending a hand to bring this book to reality include: HP Consulting and Integration, HP Software R&D, HP Software Products and Marketing.

While naming individuals risks inadvertently leaving out some names, we'd be remiss if we failed to mention the following people: Arya Barirani, Kim Dinerman, Wolfram Fischer, Ian Miller, Jeff Morgan, Judy Perez, Erik Peterson, Lee Estrin, Rajesh Radhakrishnan, Andrew Redwood, Jonathan Rende, Klaus Schmelzeisen, Kate Whalen, and Patrick Wolf.

Christian Huitema, who showed us what smart programming is, Hubert Tardieu and Ray Foulkes who gave us a lot of opportunities to verify that non-functional testing is an art.

We had no idea what it takes to put a book together and we've learned a lot from the Oak Hill team, so big thanks to Beverly Hanly, Linda Gallagher, Mary Rosberg, and Amy Guzules for all their help and guidance — we would have been lost without you.

Last and perhaps most important of all - behind every author stands a very supportive family. Sincere thanks go to Petra Harren, Jennifer Sarbiewski, and Claire, Agathe, and Margot Zahm for their love, support, and understanding throughout this project.

Andreas Golze

Mark Sarbiewski

Alain Zahm

Introduction

The word *testing* has many meanings. Teachers test their students to see how much they've learned, small children test the taste and feel of almost anything by putting things in their mouths, and scientists test the strength of materials to see how far they can be stressed before they break. (Some people say teenagers do the same thing to their parents!)

But those kinds of testing are not what we discuss in this book. Software testing is a process where we check a behavior we observe against a specified behavior the business expects.

The trial-and-error behavior that helps us learn and understand the world as children is testing without understanding the expected result.

Both methods of testing have elements in common. In both methods, we want to find out what happens if we're using something in a specific way. The primary difference is that in software testing, the tester should know what behavior to expect as defined by the business requirements. We agree on this defined, expected behavior and any user can observe this behavior.

Today, we see folks in the IT industry still confusing these two concepts of testing. Often, two groups of people are doing software testing:

- The developers or engineers who build the software application want to make sure the final product works as they intended. The testing is done from an IT or technical perspective without relating back to the business.

- The end users who will be using the final product in their jobs, in many cases, do ad hoc testing based on their day-to-day work experience. They make assumptions of how the application should work that come from their individual needs and ideas. Their approach is more trial-and-error than systemized testing — it's often ineffective and creates a lot of rework.

If each group is testing based on their needs and ideas, who's testing for the business outcomes? Who validates that the application will meet business requirements? Who mitigates the risk of failure of a software application in production?

Software testing, like software development, is a profession. Testers need to master proven techniques. Organizations like the British Computer Society and the International Software Testing Qualifications Board (ISTQB) have begun building standardized training and granting testing certification levels.

Like developers, software testers are a special breed with unique talents that can bridge the gap between the business and IT. They must have technical skills coupled with a business mentality. To build a professional test team and do testing with rigor, not by trial and error, takes time and money. For most companies using IT as the backbone for their business, time and money are the two things that are not readily available.

We, along with our colleagues, have consulted with thousands of customers on quality and testing and have seen the same issues time after time. In this book, we present a pragmatic solution to help address some of these challenges.

Our goal is not to write a comprehensive book on testing or advanced testing theory. We're showing you practical solutions, based on implementation experience. If we can help organizations solve some of their most important quality challenges quickly, we have succeeded in what we've set out to achieve here.

In this book, we address fundamental questions around testing from a business perspective.

- In Chapter 1, we examine why testing is so important to a successful product launch.

- In Chapter 2, we discuss how we know what to test and how to determine that testing has met its objectives.

- In Chapters 3 and 4, we present efficient, effective methods of software test design, which is based on equivalence partitioning.

- In Chapter 5, we define practical implementation strategies for optimizing software testing, and we show how to prioritize testing tasks and which parts of testing should be automated.

- In Chapter 6, we describe the non-functional test activities that complement the functional tests and are often underestimated when planning and preparing the test activities.

- In Chapter 7, we focus on security testing, a non-functional test stage, but one that is critical enough to devote a chapter to it.

- In Chapter 8, we focus on the organizational and process requirements for effective outsourcing. With the correct approach, you'll be able to effectively move parts of the described testing activities to off-shore or near-shore facilities.

- In Chapter 9, we give you a SUCCESSFUL approach to measuring and using key performance indicators.

- The appendices contain technical details, tips, tricks, and guidelines for those who want to go further with these concepts and begin to implement them.

Throughout this book, we use the phrase *business function(s)* to define a set of discrete end-user steps that constitute a basic business activity such as "log in," "search for a flight," or "register user." In some application environments the terms, *process steps* or *work steps* may be used instead.

We hope you gain a new business perspective on software testing and find some practical guidance for implementing quality improvements within your organization.

We might say, "Enjoy!", but we know that what you'll really enjoy is the confidence that you know how to move through your software development cycle in the most efficient, cost-effective way — and that you know your customers will be satisfied at the end of it. We will share this win-win process with you.

Chapter 1

What Is the Big Deal About Testing?

"Time waste differs from material waste in that there can be no salvage. The easiest of all wastes and the hardest to correct is the waste of time, because wasted time does not litter the floor like wasted material."
-Henry Ford

This book is about saving time. The work we've done in the IT industry for several years has taught us that professional testing can help a business save a significant amount of money on product development, reduce time to market, and gain satisfied customers.

Finding defects early in the development process makes for a product development cycle that satisfies the business stakeholders and the customers — we can vouch for that.

In manufacturing, for instance, a perfect example of the approach we favor is Toyota's. In a huge departure from the hallowed big three U.S. automakers, Toyota aligned its business requirements with its users.

- They test a cup holder like a user would, not like a designer.

- Any person on the manufacturing floor can stop the entire manufacturing process if they notice something is not right.

- Everybody on the assembly line is a quality checker.

- When a problem is spotted early, it's a lot cheaper to fix at that point, instead of cranking out a bunch of flawed cars and later having to rework the design, or possibly even do a recall.

The HP Quality Model was born out of the question, "How can we save IT costs for testing and quality management?"

To find the answer, we followed the approach made popular by Taiichi Ohno, inventor of the Toyota Quality System, and others. The 5-Why method asks five questions that help lead us down the right path.

First, we asked: **Why is IT so expensive, when hardware costs are dropping and development technologies have improved developer productivity?**

We found that despite the advancements in IT process and technology, IT projects are becoming more complex and they almost always run out of time. When time is short, people tend to sacrifice the quality of the product.

The Standish Report over the past 15 years shows the rate of successful projects (that is, under budget and on time) is below 30 percent (Figure 1). The advancements haven't lowered the cost. On the contrary, with more complexity, the need for proper planning and project management is greater.

When budget and time constraints dictate the project parameters, functionality and quality get the short end of the stick.

Success of IT Projects

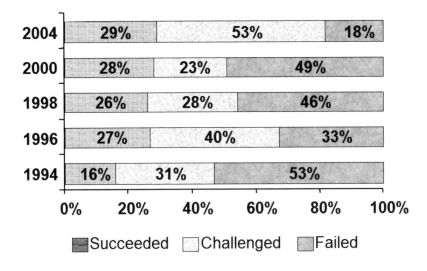

Figure 1: IT project success rate has changed over the past 10 years

To learn why the success rate is so low, we wondered: **Why were the successful projects successful?**

The Standish group also collected data on success factors, asking respondents what contributed to their project's success. Executive support and user involvement were high on the list. Here are the other factors that figured in project success.

- Executive support (18%)
- User involvement (16%)
- Experienced project manager (14%)
- Clear business objectives (12%)
- Minimized scope (10%)
- Standard software infrastructure (8%)
- Firm basic requirements (6%)

- Reliable estimates (5%)
- Other criteria (5%)

While we expected to see executive support and experienced project management, we were interested in other noteworthy elements like user involvement, clear business objectives, and firm basic requirements on the list.

All three of those factors have to do with the end user or the business, which leads us to the next question: **Why is user involvement so important?**

The answer lies in the following statistics (Figure 2), based on a 2002 study conducted by the National Institute of Science and Technology (NIST).

Understanding Defects

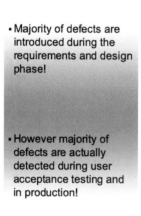

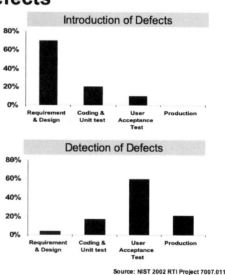

Figure 2: Comparison of where defects are introduced against where they are discovered

Figure 2 shows that most defects are introduced in the requirements phase of the traditional software development lifecycle (SDLC).

Defects in this phase happen mostly because the requirements themselves are incomplete, ambiguous, or contradictory.

When unclear requirements are translated into developers' technical specifications, misalignment of the original ambiguous business requirement and misinterpreted technical specification results in significant rework. (Interestingly, the same people who created the requirements and introduced problems in the requirements phase couldn't see their mistakes until the user acceptance phase, when they could spot them.)

So, we recommend as a best practice for those people creating requirements — double-check initial requirements for ambiguity, contradictions, and incompleteness.

This effect is not limited to software. The following example shows what can happen in situations where people omit necessary details — they have a clear idea of what they want and have made preconceived assumptions, but neglect to communicate the specifics of what they require.

I WANT SOMETHING TO GET ME ACROSS TOWN IN THE SHORTEST TIME.

The whole process begins when somebody needs something —
in this case a means of transport (the product) — and expresses
an expectation (the requirement).

The contractor asks no questions because he has a picture in his
mind of what the customer wants. Now, the contractor has
made an assumption without checking with the customer.
We're clearly missing some communication — a requirement
proof point here.

The building process starts and soon, the contractor hands the
product over to the customer for acceptance.

BUT I DON'T WANT TO GET WET!
AND HOW AM I GOING TO CARRY MY BRIEFCASE?

During the acceptance phase, the customer rejects the product
because important features are missing, and more requirements are added. Instead of starting from scratch, the developer tries to incorporate the new features into the existing
construction.

At this point, people rarely go back to their initial assumption (in this case, that the customer needs a bicycle) to find out whether the additional information (the customer doesn't want to get wet and needs to carry a briefcase) means the whole design should be reconsidered.

The reason seems to be that we make decisions based on our own perspective of the situation, rather than use a mechanism that would help obtain a more complete picture. As a result, we attempt to solve the problem without solving the problem.

Despite all efforts to the contrary, we've got an unhappy customer along with a wasted investment into something that doesn't solve the problem.

After more iterations, the solution that the contractor comes up with will be more what the customer originally wanted and the problem is solved. But taking the time to sort that out in today's dynamic marketplace means we have compromised:

- Time to market
- Cost efficiency
- Efficiency of the solution

Applying this common example to the concepts of software development, we come to the next question: **Why is the late discovery of defects a major concern, as long as defects are detected and fixed?**

The answer lies in the cost of fixing defects in various stages of the SDLC (Figure 3).

Assessing Cost of Defects

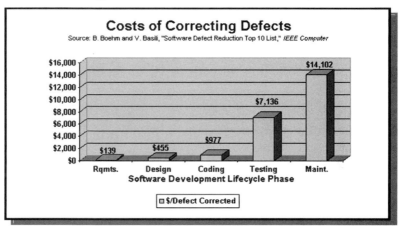

This industry average is used as a baseline for arriving at cost savings

Industry References: 3 B. Boehm and V. Basili, "Software Defect Reduction Top 10 List,"
IEEE Computer, IEEE Computer Society, Vol. 34, No. 1, January 2001, pp. 135-137.

Figure 3: The cost of correcting defects increases dramatically as we move toward the end of the SDLC

If we are complacent, neglecting to identify defects introduced in the requirements phase until we get to user acceptance testing, we lose approximately $7,000 per defect. This quickly adds up to significant numbers. It also results in the failure of many IT projects when most of the budget for the project is already spent and a huge additional monetary outlay is needed toward the end of the project.

In our bicycle/car example, all the extra work and investment was for something essentially useless to the business. In a business situation, if we consider other indirect costs that crop up, from added time-to-market and increased project risk, the cost can really break a business.

This leads to the final question: **Why can't we make use of this knowledge to improve the testing process?**

To answer that question let's first look at some testing definitions:

> **Testing is about finding defects, bugs, or flaws.**

This is true for software, as well as for all other products built
to suit specific needs. Testing is done by everyone all the time,
so why bother?

If we start looking at the testing process more carefully, we find
that in most cases, testing is not just about finding defects, but
also about knowing whether a product meets business expectations.

> **Testing is to determine if a product meets
> business expectations.**

Although this sounds pretty much the same, there is a fundamental difference. A defect is any flaw or imperfection in a
software product or process. This implies that a definition of
the perfect working product has been made and is clear to all
stakeholders. It's not a defect just because the expectations of
an individual tester have not been met.

Unfortunately, intuitive testing based on undocumented expectations is a common approach in the industry today. This testing approach is limited because it only works with the
completed product and does not allow testing to be done early
enough in the SDLC or in parallel with development.

The answer to the last question is that we can't improve the
testing process using this knowledge because in today's market, IT often dominates discussions around product expectations and defines the desired functionality around
technological aspects rather than business needs. Therefore,
the testing process is often misaligned with the needs of the
business or ideal business outcomes.

> The HP Quality Model is a pragmatic approach to software testing that aligns IT with business outcomes.

Quality Goals and Test Phases

To build meaningful and concise tests, we need to define requirements that describe the system behavior we anticipate. But that alone would not be enough to specify the intensity or the coverage needed for the tests to meet the end users' quality goals.

Quality goals are non-functional requirements. Typically in IT projects, we use these quality goals:

- **Adaptability** — How easily software can be modified to meet new requirements.

- **Maintainability** — How easily a component can be modified to correct faults, improve performance or other attributes, or adapt to a changed environment.

- **Modularity** — How much of a system or computer program is composed of discrete components and a change to one component has minimal impact on other components.

- **Generality** — The breadth of applicability of the component.

- **Portability** — How easily a system or component can be transferred from one hardware or software environment to another.

- **Reliability** — The ability of a component to perform its required functions under stated conditions for a specified period of time.

- **Correctness** — How free a component is from faults in its specification, design, and implementation. It is also how well a component meets specified requirements or user needs and expectations. And, it's the ability of a component to produce specified outputs when given specified inputs, and the extent to which they match or satisfy the requirements.

- **Completeness** — How well the component implements all required capabilities.

- **Efficiency** — How well a component performs its designated functions using minimal resources.

- **Understandability** — How clear the meaning of a software component is to the user.

- **Performance** — How well the article under test (AUT) meets the performance needs of the user. Performance may be a measure of throughput, response time, transaction or data volume, or any other related measure.

- **Security** — How well the system as a whole is protected from unauthorized access, disclosure, use disruption, modification, and destruction.

- **Availability** — The degree to which a system or component is operational when required for use.

- **Scalability** — How easily a system or component can handle growing amounts of work in a graceful manner; or the criteria to readily enlarge the capacity of a system vertically or horizontally.

Obviously it is not possible to test against all the different goals in one step. So testing is usually conducted using test phases in a phased approach. Each test phase concentrates on phase-specific quality goals and requires a different level of readiness of the product.

This phased approach is a common practice in engineering and is done to assure the quality of a single unit, before it is verified as an integrated unit to other units. The positive effects are obvious:

- When you discover an error before getting too far down the production line, it pays off in tremendous cost savings.

- It's easy to troubleshoot a product or process, or do root-cause analysis, when each element has been tested. (For instance, if you're building a brick wall, each brick has been tested before being placed in the wall so you know the problem is in the wall structure — you don't have to test the bricks again.)

- You enter every integration step with a known quality of the components (the bricks).

- Testing is easier because the functionality to be tested is limited to the component to be tested.

The test phases build on each other and are defined in such a way that testing can be done as early as possible in the SDLC. Because cost efficiency is crucial, it typically does not make sense to enter a test phase before the previous phase has met its exit criteria. For example, it may not be effective to do Performance testing before Unit testing is complete.

The prerequisite for each test phase is that the preceding test phase was executed successfully to a certain extent. The entry and exit criteria used for each test phase are called quality gates. They are introduced at the beginning and end of each phase and determine the success of the test phases.

Quality goals are requirements that describe the quality characteristics of a software product. Because different people may be involved, and the timing and the nature of the tests to be conducted are different, we divide up the test phases, as you can see in Figure 4.

HP Quality Methodology (STLC)

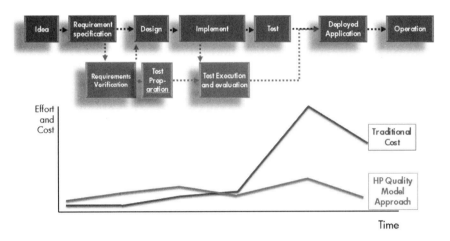

Figure 4: HP Quality Model

In the HP Quality Model, we recommend the following test phases:

Requirements Verification

In the Requirements Verification phase, the end user adds acceptance criteria to each requirement in order to answer the question, "What would make me sign off on this requirement?" The acceptance criteria needs to:

- Validate the completeness and correctness of the requirements.

- Associate the requirements with the business functions.

- Eliminate ambiguities.

- Validate that the result of each requirement is testable.

- Identify the business functions that are changed during this project (maintenance projects only).

Unit Test

The Unit Test is a white-box test conducted by the developers to find out whether the application is stable and completely implemented from a developer's perspective. (We look into white-box and black-box testing later in this chapter.)

Unit testing validates that a particular module of source code is working as the developer intended. A developer conducts the testing, not an end user. A unit has to be executable and the developer uses a debugger or self-developed tools to find out whether the code meets his expectations and the technical specification.

Integration Test

The Integration Test phase has two stages:

- **Business Function Test** — Business Function testing is the first black-box test stage where the functionality of each business function is tested against the requirements.

- **Business Process Test** — Business Process testing checks the business process end-to-end inside the application and focuses on the correct implementation of the interfaces between the business functions.

System Test

The System Test is conducted on a complete, integrated system to evaluate the entire system's compliance with its specified business requirements. System testing falls within the scope of black-box testing, and as such, should require no knowledge of the inner design of the code or logic.

Performance Test

The Performance Test determines the performance and scalability of some aspect of a system — how it performs under a real-world workload. This test may measure throughput, volume limits, transaction time, or any other similar metrics.

User Acceptance Test

The User Acceptance Test (UAT) is done by users or their representatives on a new or changed information system. If the system behaves according to their expectations, the user acceptance testers approve deploying the system. Cosmetic and other small changes may still be required as a result of the test, but the system is considered stable and behaving according to requirements.

Operational Readiness Test

The Operational Readiness Test is the final phase of testing performed on the prospective production system. This test is scheduled and conducted as a part of the production go-live plan. It is to be executed after all other cutover activities are complete, and prior to any go/no-go considerations. The Operational Readiness Test Summary Report is the final business acceptance signoff.

Each test phase requires a particular completeness of the components to be tested. These components have to be executed in a certain sequence, which is synchronized with the progress of the development team. The test phases are repeated for every release of the software and they define the software test lifecycle — a parallel process with the SDLC, but the two are also integrated (Figure 5).

Software Test Lifecycle

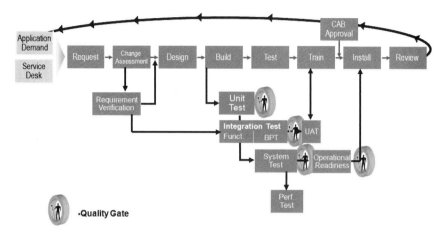

Figure 5: The software test lifecycle is shown running parallel to and integrated with the SDLC

Case Study: Flight Application

We'll illustrate how the phased approach is applied by examining the operation of a web-based portal that allows customers to book airline flights.

The portal is an easy-to-use, straightforward solution that allows customers to search, select, and book flights in the flight database. The system interfaces with the centralized booking system based on the Systems, Applications, and Products in the Data Processing (enterprise resource planning [ERP]) financial module.

Customers have to register before they can use the system. The customer-related information is stored in the centralized customer relationship management (CRM) system, along with users' passwords.

The following functions are needed:

- Log in
- Log out
- Register
- Search flight
- Book flight

Requirements Verification

The prerequisite for the Requirements Verification phase is broken down into logical business functions (Figure 6).

Functional Decomposition (example)

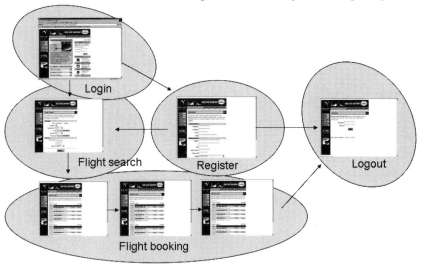

Figure 6: The business process is broken down into business functions

The Requirements Verification phase documents the acceptance criteria for each requirement of each separate business function.

Suppose one requirement for the business function LOGIN is: "The user has to enter a username and a password. By pressing a <LOG IN> button or ENTER on the keyboard, the validation of username and password should start."

The acceptance criteria for that requirement could be:

- If a username without a password is entered, an error message is displayed.

- If the username and the password are a correct combination, the system shows the flight-search screen.

- If the username and the password are not a valid combination, an error message is displayed.

Ideally, the business analyst or business user writing the acceptance criteria identifies missing information and ambiguities in the requirements, documents those as defects, and hands them over to the development team.

Possible quality gates for the Requirements Verification phase are:

- One hundred percent of the requirements have at least one documented acceptance criterion (such as the online flight booking).

- We have divided the application into business functions and prioritized each business function according to the quality needed to meet the business goal of allowing the user to book a flight online.

Unit Test

Unit testing is part of the development lifecycle, so we don't make specific recommendations for this phase in our airline booking example.

However, we need to agree on the quality gates for the Unit Test, because it defines the quality level we can expect when the software is handed over. In other words, if the software does not meet the defined criteria, the test team will not accept it for the Integration Test.

Possible quality gates for the Unit Test are:

- **Statement Coverage** — Has each line of the source code been executed and tested?

- **Condition Coverage** — Has each evaluation point (such as a true/false decision) been executed and tested?

- **Path Coverage** — Has every possible route through a given part of the code been executed and tested?

Integration Test

During the Integration Test we first look at the implementation of each business function. After we validate that the business function is functioning correctly, we can move to the next phase, the various combinations of business functions.

Business Function Test

We're testing these business functions in our example applications:

- Log in
- Log out
- Register
- Flight search
- Flight booking

We test each function independently as soon as it has passed the Unit Test, using various approaches to complete the function test. We suggest using equivalence partitioning for the test case development (we'll explain more in Chapters 4 and 5).

Regardless of the applied methodology, the quality gates need to be defined and met.

Possible quality gates for the Business Function Test are:

- All planned test cases have been executed.
- All incidents have been logged as defects.

- All identified defects have been resolved. ("Resolved" means they're either closed or a decision has been made to delay the closing.)

Business Process Test

When it comes to the Business Process Test, we want to make sure to test the various possible business function sequences. In our flight-booking example, the possible process is shown in Figure 7.

Business Process (example)

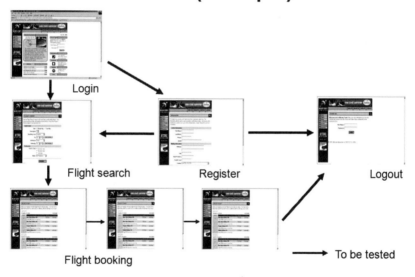

Figure 7: Sample business process for a flights application

It's important to test each possible connection between the business functions once. The focus is the transition from one business function to the next and not the functional correctness of the single business function (addressed during the Business Function Test).

Possible quality gates for the Business Process Test might be:

- All end-to-end processes can be executed.
- A workaround exists for all defects found.

System Test

During the System Test, each individual application should have passed the quality gates for the Integration Test. The System Test often involves large and complex environments with multiple independent applications working together to support a business process (Figure 8).

Flight System Architecture

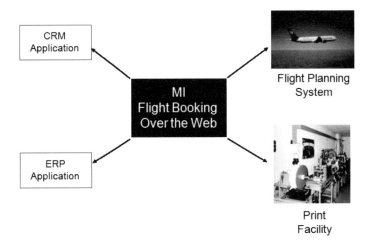

Figure 8: A flight-booking system is supported by multiple independent applications

The System Test makes sure various applications work together as the business process requires — flight planning, ticketing, customer relations. The focus of the System Test is:

■ **Functional correctness** — All interfacing applications are in place and the application functions correctly in the defined environment.

■ **Reliability** — The system can perform and maintain its functions in routine circumstances, as well as in hostile or unexpected circumstances.

- **Accessibility** — A system is usable by as many people as possible with modification.

Possible quality gates for the System Test are:

- All end-to-end processes can be executed.

- No severe defects exist.

Performance Test

The Performance Test helps us:

- Demonstrate that the system meets performance criteria.

- Compare two systems to find which performs better.

- Measure which parts of the system or workload cause the system to perform badly.

When troubleshooting, software engineers use tools such as profilers to measure which parts of a device or software contribute most to the poor performance or to establish throughput levels (and thresholds) to maintain acceptable response time.

> The later a performance defect is detected, the higher the cost of remediation.

When Performance testing begins at the inception of the development project and extends through to deployment, you have a better chance of catching defects early and thereby saving money and time that would otherwise have to be budgeted to fix problems down the line.

In Chapter 6, we focus on the different aspects of the Performance Test and describe how it can be performed throughout the product lifecycle.

User Acceptance Test

When users are satisfied that the business functional specifications and business requirements have been met, system sign-off and release can take place. The User Acceptance Test (UAT) phase involves turning loose a number of real end users to try the system, using it as they would in real life to accomplish whatever task the system is designed for.

The goal is to make sure that the end users are comfortable with the system they will be working with and that all their requirements are met.

Often a team will leverage training of the end users as a means to perform User Acceptance testing. In our flight example, we might have reservation agents go through the system and make flight reservations and help identify any issues in the flight system.

The quality gate for the UAT is the end-user sign-off.

Operational Readiness Test

The project requirements and design specification documents clearly define the expectations for systems operational readiness. We've been aware of operational readiness levels while we've conducted previous testing phases (Unit, System, Integration, Performance, and UAT).

Operational Readiness testing ensures that the system we are about to deliver has the appropriate production data loaded, is ready to communicate with required external systems, and is ready to run the necessary regular batch processes, while meeting any specific security and compliance requirements.

For the flight application, we might check to make sure that the flight data is being populated correctly, that billing processes that use an external system are working, and that the ticket purchase process is done through secure channels so users are not worried about sharing their private information.

This test phase is the last check of the production system for operational readiness before the system go-live point. This phase should be a part of the Project Implementation Plan.

Key elements of Operational Readiness testing are:

- End-user setup
- Role definitions and requirements
- Security allocations and passwords
- End-to-end connectivity verification
- Production data verification
- Core business functionality verification
- Removable or read-only system interaction
- Application monitoring tool verification
- Call/Service center support setup
- Support documentation

The quality gates for the Operational Readiness Test are normally defined by the operations team or, if the operations task is outsourced, these quality gates can be defined by a combination of the service providers that host the application and the internal operations team.

Test Concepts and Techniques

Many test techniques have been developed over the years for the different test phases, but there are two basic types of test: The white-box test and the black-box test.

White-Box Testing

White-box testing is also known as clear-box testing, glass-box testing, or structural testing. The term *white box* (or glass box) indicates that the tester knows the code used to execute certain functionality.

In software testing, it's usually a programmer that performs white-box tests. Often, multiple programmers will write tests based on certain code to gain various perspectives on possible outcomes.

In the fields of computer programming, software engineering, and software testing, white-box testing is used to check that the outputs of a program, given certain inputs, conform to the structural specifications of the program. In electrical hardware testing, every node in a circuit may be probed and measured (in-circuit test, or ICT).

The most common techniques and approaches used in white-box testing are syntax testing, statement testing, branch/decision testing, data flow testing, branch condition testing, branch condition combination testing, and modified condition decision testing. (For detailed descriptions of these test techniques, see Appendix A.)

Black-Box Testing

In white-box testing we saw that the tester — usually the developer — had insight into how the application was developed. However, when a third-party or impartial tester does not know how the programs were developed, they can conduct black-box testing.

In computer programming, software engineering, and software testing, we use black-box testing (also known as concrete box or functional testing) to check that the outputs of a program, given certain inputs, conform to the functional specification of the program. In electrical hardware testing, we black-box test the specifications of the interface between the device and application circuit.

The term *black box* indicates that the tester does not examine the internal implementation of the program being executed. For this reason, black-box testing is not normally carried out by the programmer. In most engineering firms, one group does design work and a separate group does the testing.

The most common techniques and approaches used in black-box testing are the smoke test, equivalence partitioning, boundary value analysis, and user input validation. (For detailed descriptions of these tests techniques, see Appendix A.)

Wrapping Up

By now, you can see how testing can help your company's bottom line in a new product release, saving you considerable money by catching flaws early in the process and reducing rework for your team.

We've showed you how our approach works in the software field, but you can apply this method in most any industry and it's an excellent way to troubleshoot internal business processes.

> By setting out clear requirements that align with your business goals, you'll save yourself some headaches and preserve good customer relations.

Our experiences with other test methodologies have led us to adopt an approach to test design that departs somewhat from traditional testing. It's aligned with business outcomes and is focused on the end-user experience — testing to make sure the customer will have a satisfactory experience, not just that developers see the results they expect.

But before we start testing, we have to better understand what to test.

Chapter 2

Testing the Business Requirements: Start at the Root of the Problem

The HP Quality Model attacks the primary source of application defects: requirements. According to the United States National Institute of Standards and Technology, incomplete, vague, or conflicting requirements typically cause a whopping 70 percent of an application's defects.

Using our structured approach to testing the requirements, you can find and correct these problems before development — or even design — begins.

> Clear requirements improve the final quality, reduce time to complete the project, and lower the cost of project delivery.

Technically, testing is about finding defects, but it's also about making sure the requirements are met.

Getting clearly articulated requirements can be difficult. We need the users' perspective, and the users are often too busy to define precisely what they need.

Remember that picture from Chapter 1 where the user wants a car but gets a bicycle? The too-busy user created more work for the company and had to expend more effort himself. After getting the bicycle, he had to explain the problem he was trying to solve in more detail and then wait longer for a better solution.

> The time not taken to define what's needed at the beginning is not saved. Instead, more time is spent having to refine an incomplete requirement in order to get a satisfactory solution.

Various techniques exist for getting complete requirements early, but one thing is sure: telling busy users that it's in their best interest— even though it is — is rarely a successful strategy. Asking, telling, or demanding may work, but usually it's not effective.

Because good test design depends on having clear requirements, we need a successful strategy to get them in place.

> The best route to obtaining clear requirements leverages the organization's culture and politics.

Some organizations solve the "busy user" problem by creating a role — often called a business analyst — that represents the users' application needs. When the test results come in, you ask the user or business analyst if the outcome was successful: "Is this what you wanted?"

The user already has a picture in mind about what success looks like. What if we ask at the start how the user will recognize success? The answers — successful-outcome statements — are a very good way to expand the requirements.

While this is a valuable technique, it doesn't help when requirements are missing, so how can we assure completeness?

Perhaps the best way to come up with complete requirements is through formal verification. Software engineers have used this process for many years. It was developed by Michael Fagan in the 1970s and many documents are available to describe the process. (See, for example, *Software Formal Inspections Guidebook*, published by NASA as NASA-GB-A302.)

We describe another solution, equivalence partitioning, in Chapter 3. The advantage of this approach is that the end user is supported when structuring the required functionality and when describing requirements without gaps or ambiguities.

So far we've used the term "requirements" very generally, but there are many types of requirements:

- End-user requirements
- Operational requirements
- Platform requirements
- Corporate requirements
- Compliance requirements
- Software requirements, or functional requirements

We won't go into these in depth, other than to say that they all need to be considered. Unfortunately, most people only consider end-user requirements in their project planning.

Software requirements (last on the list) are often called specifications. There's an important distinction between end-user requirements and specifications:

> End-user requirements address the problem to be solved.
> Specifications describe a solution to the problem.

If the contractor had prepared a specification in our car-vs.-bicycle example and presented it to the user, the problem would have been cleared up well before the bicycle was built, umbrella and all.

Let's focus on exploring the relationship between the requirements and testing. (Plenty of texts discuss best practices for requirements gathering; for example, *Mastering the Requirements Process* by James and Suzanne Robertson.)

Requirements are the means of communication between business and IT. Because of their importance in the HP Quality Model, we include Requirements Verification as a test phase.

During the Requirements Verification phase, we take the following steps:

1. Build a common reference for business analysts and IT.
2. Document the separate business functions
3. Link the requirements with the common reference.
4. Add proof points to each requirement.

Build a Common Reference

We start with the end user's perspective. We need to get the end user to articulate the business functions he uses during work hours. This approach is independent of whether we're modifying software that is already in place or we're building a new system from scratch.

First we make a list of the business functions or activities the end user performs. We'll group them to handle them easier.

We break down and separate the functions with representatives of the business side and the requirements engineer. Consider the following guidelines:

A business function supports a basic end-user activity — it's a step in the business process. The business function has a testable result.

Thumb rules for breaking down the application into business functions are:

- Each use case, or basic end-user activity, is a business function.

- If a group of use cases is very similar, group them together to form one business function.

- If a use case is very large or very complex, split it into two or more business functions.

- To completely test a single business function, we should need no more than 30 to 40 positive test cases.

Adapt those guidelines and interpret them according to the project environment. Usually projects using object-oriented methodology have a different view on functionality than projects using structured analysis and design.

However, keep in mind that the functionality that the business needs in order to support its work is independent from the underlying methodology. We can derive the business functionality using this guideline.

Here's a sample application that keeps customer contact information. In a given application environment, the functional breakdown would look like Table 1.

Customer Contact
Incoming customer contact
Outgoing customer contact
Create customer
Identify customer
Register interaction
Change/maintain customer information
Customer message

Table 1: Sample business functions of a customer contact application

Document the Separate Business Functions

To document the business function breakdown, we build requirements into a tree structure. One way this can be implemented is in the HP Quality Center software (for more information, see Appendix B). The tree structure has the basic elements shown in Figure 9.

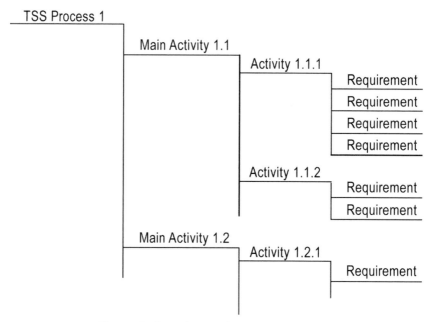

Figure 9: Sample requirements structure

For our customer contact example, the structure would look like Figure 10.

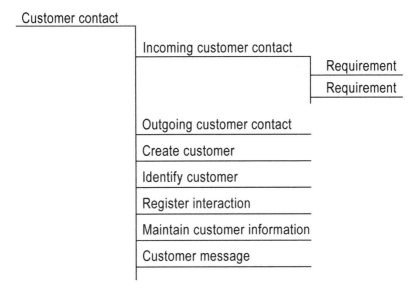

Figure 10: Customer contact requirements structure

Link Requirements into the Structure

Most companies document requirements independently, without structure, in tools like Word, Excel, Lotus Notes, or Outlook. In this step, we link the requirement assets with the appropriate business functions. This way, we create a direct mapping between the structure of the business activity from the business perspective and the detailed requirements for each of the business functions.

We can use this mapping for reporting and analysis purposes to find out which business areas are covered by requirements and which are not.

Define Proof Points

Most requirements testing approaches use review techniques where people work through the written requirement to find the issues and complete them. These techniques can be very effective at the beginning of a project to create a new software application.

However, modifying existing software is much more common than creating brand-new applications from scratch. For requirements based on changes, we introduce "proof points." These are simple statements of exactly how one would recognize that a requirement has been met. (Proof points can, of course, be used for new software applications as well.)

Think about what would make an end user sign off on this requirement. For example, if our requirement is to build a house, we ask ourselves what list of items would allow us to sign off that the house is complete. Do we want a four-sided brick house? Do we need a kitchen with stainless steel appliances?

> When you think of the questions that would allow you to accept and sign off on the requirement, it will help you create more relevant proof points.

For every requirement, a specific measure of compliance needs to be in place, and you must be able to demonstrate that the requirement has been met. That is, you must be able to perform a test concerning that requirement.

The process is this: Each requirement must have within it a statement of the acceptance criteria. We then translate the product requirement and acceptance criteria into a test requirement, which tells precisely how to determine if the requirement has been met.

Using our customer contact example, let's extend the requirements tree a bit.

Customer Contact

- Incoming contact
  - Requirement 1: display customer ID from incoming telephone number.
  - Requirement 2: system automatically answers the call within four rings.

Stated this way, two things emerge. First, it is relatively easy to create proof points based on questions:

- What would satisfy the requirement here?
- Are we okay with any customer ID displayed?
- Do we need the customer ID to be the telephone number?
- Can we display something other than the ID?
- Will we accept the system answering calls with more than four rings?
- What about no rings?
- Are we okay if the system does not automatically answer the phone?

By asking these questions, we come up with the following proof points:

- Correct customer ID is based on the telephone number.
- Only a customer ID is displayed.
- The call has to be answered automatically.
- The call has to be answered within four rings.

Then another question emerges: What if the call comes from an unrecognized number? This question can lead us to additional requirements and show us that we need additional tests.

Requirements are usually hierarchical in nature, going from the general to the specific. We can lay these out in a tree structure as shown in Figure 10, with all related requirements gathered together in each branch of the tree. The requirements structure guides the test-plan creation and the test-plan tree matches the requirements tree.

> The execution plan for any test uses the test-requirements tree overlaid with the priority of each of the requirements, so the testing focuses on the most important items first.

We determine the priority using the business risk calculations, which we will discuss in detail in Chapter 5, along with technical IT considerations. Although some elements may not be high priority from a business perspective, they may be vital for the proper execution of the business functions. For example, most business people are not so much interested in network protocols, but without success in this area, the business processes could fail.

Because we base the test plan on the requirements, it becomes a simple matter to understand the status of any requirement during the course of the test. It's possible to look for a specific requirement, for example, to be a certain percentage complete.

We can also report on the percentage of requirements the test cases have covered. Determining the business risks associated with testing is possible by analyzing how well we've covered the requirements.

One way of implementing this is to start with a 100 percent risk of failure at the beginning of the development lifecycle. As tests cover the requirements and are passed, we lower the risk, until ideally the risk becomes zero before we make the go-live decision.

> We present the test status in terms that make sense to the business users and the tests are aligned with business outcomes.

A slightly more sophisticated approach takes the priorities of the requirements into account. By prioritizing the require-ments, and aligning the testing with those priorities, we can assure that the important things are done first. That way, if, as often happens, we run out of time, we can be sure that we have reduced risk as much as possible.

Status reports then can discuss the coverage percent for High, Medium, and Low priority requirements. Of course, if the reports indicate that 100 percent of the Low priority require-ments have been tested and 0 percent of the High priority requirements have been tested, we'd have to revisit the plan-ning activity!

Now that we understand what to test and how to align what to test with the business outcomes, the next step is to design the actual tests. Many organizations do this in an ad hoc fashion. In the next chapter, we show you a more effective test design method.

Chapter 3

Test Rules:
Build the Backbone
for Effective Testing

The core of our approach is to start testing as early as possible. We do this by asking for the acceptance criteria for each requirement. For instance, in Chapter 1 we used an example of someone looking for a means of transport. His acceptance criteria might be:

- It has to be red.

- It can travel 100 miles an hour.

- It has a convertible roof.

- It looks like a Porsche Carrera.

Acceptance criteria are what we call the test rules.

Test cases, which include test rules, are the basis for all testing activities, independent of which testing phase they occur in.

A test case consists of the test rule and the test data. This differentiation is important, because the same test rule can be used with different sets of test data to form different test cases. But from a coverage perspective, these various test cases can prove or test the same functionality.

> Test case = test rule + test data
>
> Test rule = a determined operation that leads to a defined result
>
> Test data = data needed with the test rule to execute and evaluate a test

Using another example, validating a purchase order, we check the age of a purchaser, who must be 18 years or older for the purchase to be accepted. To execute the test, we need two test rules to verify the correct implementation:

- A purchaser's birth date is 18 years or more in the past
- A purchaser's birth date is less than 18 years in the past

These two test rules cover the described functionality completely, so we have 100 percent functional coverage. However, to get executable test cases, we need to add test data — in this case, birth dates -- one for each rule.

The two dates are the least amount of test data we need for functionality. We could create more dates to execute the test with, and each date would then lead to a new test case, but it would not lead to better coverage of the functionality to be tested. (Testing the same function represented by the test rule with more data points makes sense, because it builds more confidence for the technical implementation and increases the data coverage of the test, but it does not increase the functional coverage.)

> Functional coverage: The degree to which each business rule is executed
>
> Data coverage: The degree to which a function is executed with the possible data combinations

Because testing is always a balance between the security we want for a quality application and the effort we can afford spend, it is up to the test manager to define the quality goals for functional coverage and data coverage for the application under test.

Differentiating between test rule and test data is helpful for achieving various quality goals, and it enables managers to split the test work among the stakeholders allowing an early start for test activities.

However, this chapter is about how to get to test rules efficiently. Before we start, let's go back to an aspect of testing we discussed in Chapter 1. There, we pointed out that various quality goals are achieved through different test phases. The test rules we're developing here prove the functional correctness of the application, so they're used in these test phases:

- Requirement Verification
- Integration testing
- User Acceptance testing

The final test case could describe other test phases where it makes sense to reuse the rules, but the goal of these test rules is to verify functional correctness. (As we'll see later, we won't be able to spend the effort for test-rule development that leads to 100 percent functional coverage for all the business functions of the application. We introduce an approach that would ensure 100 percent functional coverage, but we'll discuss how this can be trimmed and so reduce the effort for the test-rule development.)

Equivalence Partitioning with Root Cause Analysis

The approach we use for test-rule determination is a combination of equivalence partitioning and root cause analysis.

Equivalence partitioning is a software-testing technique designed to:
- Reduce the number of test cases to a necessary minimum
- Select the right test cases to cover all possible scenarios

Requirements are the basis for test-rule definition. In Chapter 2, we recommended clustering the requirements, which results in what we call "business functions." These are the activities that describe the end user's steps that the application needs to support.

In the first step, the test rules are defined separately for each business function. This achieves a high level of parallelization and independence during test preparation, test execution, and test evaluation, which allows us to start testing at the earliest possible time.

To show how the approach works, let's use the example of the business function, "date."

Date is a standalone functionality that checks if the 8-digit number entered is a valid date.

- We assume the proper entry format for the date is DD MM YYYY.

- We assume that only numbers can be entered.

With this specification we proceed to the test rule definition:

STEP 1: Identifying the data entry fields

DD

MM

YYYY

STEP 2: Equivalence partitioning

Data Field Name	Data Entry	Expected Result
DD	00, 32–99	Invalid date
	00–28	Invalid date
	29	Depends
	30	Depends
	31	Depends

Equivalence partitioning is based on the whole set of data that's possible to enter into the field. In the DD fields, it's the numbers from 00 to 99. Next, we split this set into subsets in which each subset has a clearly defined result with respect to the requirement.

- In our example, 00 and 32 will not be valid days, and so all members of this subset will give the result "Invalid date."

- The numbers 01-28 will always be valid dates.

- The numbers 29, 30, and 31 depend on the month and the year entered to determine whether the date is valid.

Data Field Name	Data Entry	Expected Result
MM	00, 13–99	Invalid date
	02	Depends
	01, 03, 05, 07, 08, 10, 12	Depends
	04, 06, 09, 11	Depends

The set of possible data for the MM field is again the numbers 00 to 99.

- The subset 00 and 13 - 99 will result in an "Invalid date" response, and the rest will result in "Depends."

- With some subject matter knowledge, we can split this subset even further:

  - February (02) can be 28 or 29, depending on whether it occurs in a leap year.

  - All other months can be split into two subsets, one with 30-day months and the other with 31-day months.

The subject matter knowledge we used in this case is important for splitting the data into further subsets. So, whenever you split data into subsets with a common expected result, you should get input from the end user -- in most cases you'll gain information that's not documented in the requirement.

Data Field Name	Data Entry	Expected Result
YYYY	Leap year	Depends
	Non-leap year	Depends

The YYYY field is split into two subsets:

- All the leap years
- All the non-leap years

You'll notice there are no invalid years. Often, dates before 1900 would be considered invalid, but our specification has no such rule. However, we could discuss this with the business users of the application.

If we put all this together, we come to the following overview:

Data Field Name	Data Entry	Expected Result
DD	00, 32–99	Invalid date
	00–28	Invalid date
	29	Depends
	30	Depends
	31	Depends
MM	00, 13–99	Invalid date
	02	Depends
	01, 03, 05, 07, 08, 10, 12	Depends
	04, 06, 09, 11	Depends
YYYY	Leap year	Depends
	Non-leap year	Depends

STEP 3: Resolving the dependencies

When we specify the expected result for each subset, we sometimes need more information before we can determine that
result. We've indicated the demand for more information by
entering "Depends" in the expected result field. We'll collect
information for the fields that need to be evaluated, so we can
determine the expected result.

In our *date* example, this leads to the following result:

Data Field Name	Data Entry	Expected Result
DD	29	Depends
	30	Depends
	31	Depends
MM	02	Depends
	01, 03, 05, 07, 08, 10, 12	Depends
	04, 06, 09, 11	Depends
YYYY	Leap year	Depends
	Non-leap year	Depends

We'll consider all three data fields to determine the expected result. To limit the complexity of the test case development process, try to limit the number of subsets for data entry for each data field to the absolute minimum possible. The more subsets you select, the more test cases you have to draw from.

STEP 4: Creating combinations

To identify all possible rules that describe the dependency of the three fields (day DD, month MM, and year YYYY), we combine the three subsets of data with each other.

There are 18 combinations possible:

Data Field Name	Data Entry	Combinations																	
		1	2	3	4	5	6	7	8	9	10	11	12	13	14	15	16	17	18
DD	29	✓			✓			✓			✓			✓			✓		
	30		✓			✓			✓			✓			✓			✓	
	31			✓			✓			✓			✓			✓			✓
MM	02	✓	✓	✓							✓	✓	✓						
	01, 03, 05, 07, 08. 10, 12				✓	✓	✓							✓	✓	✓			
	04, 06, 09, 11							✓	✓	✓							✓	✓	✓
YYYY	Leap year	✓	✓	✓	✓	✓	✓	✓	✓	✓									
	Non-leap year										✓	✓	✓	✓	✓	✓	✓	✓	✓

In this matrix, we have combined each subset of each data field with the subsets of all the other data fields.

STEP 5: Adding expected results to each combination

Now we can determine the expected results for each combination. Two different results are possible:

- R1: valid date
- R2: invalid date

If we add this information to the table, we get the following:

Data Field Name	Data Entry	Combinations																	
		1	2	3	4	5	6	7	8	9	10	11	12	13	14	15	16	17	18
DD	29	✓			✓			✓			✓			✓			✓		
	30		✓			✓			✓			✓			✓			✓	
	31			✓			✓			✓			✓			✓			✓
MM	02	✓	✓	✓							✓	✓	✓						
	01, 03, 05, 07, 08, 10, 12				✓	✓	✓							✓	✓	✓			
	04, 06, 09, 11							✓	✓	✓							✓	✓	✓
YYYY	Leap year	✓	✓	✓	✓	✓	✓	✓	✓	✓									
	Non-leap year										✓	✓	✓	✓	✓	✓	✓	✓	✓
Expected result		R1	R2	R2	R1	R1	R1	R1	R1	R2	R2	R2	R2	R1	R1	R1	R1	R1	R2

Each of the columns in this matrix defines a test rule for the function date.

So, if we tested the function with a representative data combination for each column, we'd have a complete test for this dependency. However we can improve this scenario with this assumption: Rules that lead to the same result, that are only different in one data field, can be combined. The differentiation into two subsets is not necessary.

STEP 6a: Reducing the number of combinations

If we look at the different combinations, we find that some of them lead to the same results. Here's an opportunity to reduce their number by combining them. When we do this, two rules have to be obeyed to avoid a degradation in the test coverage.

- Unite only combinations that have the same expected result.

- Unite only two combinations that are different in only one data field.

To see how we apply these rules in our example:

- Look at combinations 2 and 3 in the table below: in both cases the result is R2.

- Look at the data fields only for DD: two different subsets are selected, 30 and 31.

- Look at MM: in both cases the result is 2.

- Look for the leap year in the YYYY field: if we read it a little differently, we notice that whether month 02 in a leap year has 30 or 31 days, it is always an invalid date.

So the combinations 2 and 3, shown in gray, could be reduced to one. To show this in the table, we introduce a new symbol (✗) to show that this combination is covered already.

The table for the reduction of combination 2 and 3 would then look as follows:

Data Field Name	Data Entry	Combinations																	
		1	2	3	4	5	6	7	8	9	10	11	12	13	14	15	16	17	18
DD	29	✓			✓			✓			✓			✓			✓		
	30		✓			✓			✓			✓			✓			✓	
	31			✗			✓			✓			✓			✓			✓
MM	02	✓	✓	✓							✓	✓	✓						
	01, 03, 05, 07, 08, 10, 12				✓	✓	✓							✓	✓	✓			
	04, 06, 09, 11							✓	✓	✓							✓	✓	✓
YYYY	Leap year	✓	✓	✓	✓	✓	✓	✓	✓	✓									
	Non-leap year										✓	✓	✓	✓	✓	✓	✓	✓	✓
Expected result		R1	R2	R2	R1	R1	R1	R1	R1	R2	R2	R2	R2	R1	R1	R1	R1	R1	R2

To find the combinations that can be made part of another combination, look for those with equal expected results. If two combinations are only different in one data field, they can be merged.

STEP 6b: Further reducing the number of combinations

We'll now go through all combinations and look for possible reductions:

Data Field Name	Data Entry	Combinations																	
		1	2	3	4	5	6	7	8	9	10	11	12	13	14	15	16	17	18
DD	29	✓			✓			✓			✓			✓			✓		
	30		✓			✗			✗			✗			✗			✗	
	31			✗			✗			✓			✗			✗			✓
MM	02	✓	✓	✓							✓	✓	✓						
	01, 03, 05, 07, 08. 10, 12				✓	✓	✓							✓	✓	✓			
	04, 06, 09, 11							✓	✓	✓							✓	✓	✓
YYYY	Leap year	✓			✓	✓	✓	✓	✓	✓									
	Non-leap year										✓			✓	✓	✓	✓	✓	✓
Expected result		R1	R2	R2	R1	R1	R1	R1	R1	R2	R2	R2	R2	R1	R1	R1	R1	R1	R2

- Combinations 4, 5, and 6 can be merged because every month in the second subset of MM has 31 days.

- Combinations 7 and 8 can be merged because every month in the third group of MM has 30 days.

- Combinations 10, 11, and 12 can be merged because in a non-leap year, 02 never has 29, 30, or 31 days.

- Combinations 13, 14, and 15 can be merged because every month in the second subset of MM has 31 days.

- Combinations 16 and 17 can be merged because every month in the third subset of MM has 30 days.

STEP 6c: Reducing the number of combinations still further

The result of step 6b looks as follows:

		Combinations								
Data Field Name	Data Entry	1	2	4	7	9	10	13	16	18
DD	29	✓		✓	✓			✓	✓	
	30		✓							
	31					✓	✓			✓
MM	02	✓	✓				✓			
	01, 03, 05, 07, 08. 10, 12				✓				✓	
	04, 06, 09, 11			✓		✓		✓		✓
YYYY	Leap year	✓	✓	✓	✓	✓	✓			
	Non-leap year							✓	✓	✓
Expected result		R1	R2	R1	R1	R2	R2	R1	R1	R2

The rule to merge combinations can be applied again.

Data Field Name	Data Entry	Combinations								
		1	2	4	7	9	10	13	16	18
DD	29	✓		✓	✓		✓	✓	✓	
	30		✓							
	31					✓				✓
MM	02	✓	✓				✓			
	01, 03, 05, 07, 08. 10, 12			✓				✓	✓	✓
	04, 06, 09, 11				✓	✓				
YYYY	Leap year	✓	✓	✓	✓	✓				
	Non-leap year						✓	✗	✗	✗
Expected result		R1	R2	R1	R1	R2	R2	R1	R1	R2

- Combinations 4 and 13 can be merged because every month in the second subset of MM has 31 days, which is true in leap and non-leap years.

- Combinations 7 and 16 can be merged because the third subset of MM has 30 days, which is true for leap and non-leap years.

- Combinations 9 and 18 can be merged because every month in the third subset of MM has only 30 days, so entering "31" would lead to the result invalid date, which is true in leap and non-leap years.

So finally, we have to look only for six different combinations, which represent all the business rules behind this dependency.

STEP 7: Putting it all together

Now we synthesize the results of the different steps, and that gives us the test rules that have to be executed to test the application date.

These test rules represent the complete functionality of the business function, so we have 100 percent functional coverage.

To define the test rules, we did not need the application, we just needed:

- The data that goes into the application
- The business knowledge about the functionality

		Test Rules								
Data Field Name	Data Entry	1	2	3	4	5	6	7	8	9
DD	00, 32–99	✓								
	00–28		✓	✓						
	29				✓		✓	✓		✓
	30					✓	✓	✓		
	31					✓	✓		✓	✓
MM	00, 13–99			✓						
	02	✓	✓		✓	✓				✓
	01, 03, 05, 07, 08. 10, 12	✓	✓				✓			
	04, 06, 09, 11							✓	✓	
YYYY	Leap year	✓	✓	✓	✓	✓	✓	✓	✓	
	Non-leap year	✓	✓	✓						✓
Expected result		R1	R2	R2	R2	R2	R1	R1	R2	R2

The next step will transform these test rules into test cases —
and we'll do that in the next chapter.

Chapter 4

Test Cases: Let's Get Down to the Real Stuff

In the last chapter, we learned how to systematically establish the test rules for a business function. Now we can derive the test case from those test rules, which describe the results we want to see in the test.

For instance, if we were to test the software for an ATM machine before it shipped to the customer, one test rule might be: When a customer puts a credit card into the card slot, the customer is prompted to enter a PIN number.

For test execution we need to define:

- Account number
- Name of the bank that holds the card
- Type of credit card
- Name of the account owner

And we need to ensure that the data on the card matches the data in the system. The additional information will transform the *test rule* into a *test case*.

> Test case = scenario + data used to uncover errors in the software

Depending on the environment in which the test is executed, even more information may be required, but the following elements are pretty common to all kinds of software. This information helps organize the execution of the test case:

- Preconditions
- Activities necessary for test case execution
- Expected result
- Access rights for the tester
- Knowledge of the tester
- Version of the application under test (AUT)
- Name and location of the test environment

Because we need to come up with all the required information during the test case build, we strongly recommend using a standardized approach to ensure we don't forget anything. We use a form to document each test case in our projects.

Test Case Description No.

Application under test

Name			
Version		Test user	
Test environment		Password	

Tester

Name		Execution date	
Special qualification required			

Test rule covered			

Master data

File name and location		
Load procedure		
Manual steps		

Entry data

<Field name>	<Value>	
<Field name>	<Value>	

Expected result

<Result number>	<Result description>	
<Result number>	<Result description>	

Actual result

<Result number (optional)>	<Defect number (optional)>	

Name:	Date:
Signature:	

Just as we did during the test-rule definition, we fill in the form step by step.

Step 1: Select a Test Rule

The test rules we developed in the last chapter give us the baseline we need to build the test cases. Let's assume we select test rule 1:

Data Field Name	Data Entry	1
DD	00, 32–99	✓
	00–28	
	29	
	30	
	31	
MM	00, 13–99	
	02	✓
	01, 03, 05, 07, 08, 10, 12	✓
	04, 06, 09, 11	
YYYY	Leap year	✓
	Non-leap year	✓
Expected result		R2

We can transfer the data field names and the expected result directly into the test case form. To enter data, though, we have to make a decision. Several test cases can all proof the correct implementation of test rule 1. The difference between these test cases lies in the data we select for execution.

In our example, the tester must choose from the possible values 00, 32 -99 for the DD field. Each value will lead to the same result, and so will all test cases of one rule.

The number of test cases we need to execute should be linked to the business risk assigned to this business function. (See Chapter 5.)

Based on our experience, we suggest the following strategy for test-case definition.

High-risk business functions

Select data from each group that is part of the test rule. In our example:

- DD: 00, 32-99
- MM: 02
        01, 03, 05, 07, 08, 10, 12
        04, 06, 09, 11
- YYYY: Leap year
        Non-leap year

Select all boundaries of the intervals and one random value out of the interval. In our example:

- DD: 00
        32
        99
        One value out of 32-99

Medium-risk business functions

Select data from each group that is part of the test rule. In our example:

- DD: 00, 32-99
- MM: 02
        01, 03, 05, 07, 08, 10, 12
        04, 06, 09, 11
- YYYY: Leap year
        Non-leap year

Low-risk business functions

Randomly select one set of data.

Let's assume the business function date is a high-risk business function. If so, we should have at least five test cases.

We'll document each test case using the form we introduced at the beginning of this chapter. So, after Step 1, the section "Entry Data" will be filled. In our example, the result looks like this:

Test Case Description No. 900			
Application under test			
Name			
Version		Test user	
Test environment		Password	
Tester			
Name		Execution date	
Special qualification required			
Test rule covered			
Master data			
File name and location			
Load procedure			
Manual steps			
Entry data			
DD	00		
MM	01		
YYYY	2000		
Expected result			
R900	Wrong date		

As you can see, we have numbered that test case "900." This is a convention we use to identify test cases leading to a negative result. (The complete convention for numbering can be found in Appendix D.) We strongly recommend using a convention like this — test organization is easier when the numbering of test cases, or an expected result, carries additional information.

Step 2: Specifying Master Data

Master data is the information that must be in the system to make the execution of the test case possible. The definition of master data happens in two stages. In the first stage, describe the data in a general way. Here's how this works.

Business function to be tested:

Flight booking (see Chapter 1)

Functional specification:

- A list of matching flights is displayed: The user selects a flight by clicking a radio button. (The first flight in the list is selected by default.)
- Pressing the <CONTINUE> button or ENTER on the keyboard brings up the payment screen, which gathers all relevant information for payment using a credit card.
- A billing address and a delivery address is required: The correctness of the address and the consistency is validated. If information is missing or inconsistencies are entered, an error message pointing the user to the problem is displayed.
- After the customer successfully completes the payment screen, a confirmation number is displayed.

This description is simplified, and if you try to identify all the test rules for it you'll find gaps and ambiguities, but it helps explain what we mean by master data.

Screenshot of the main data entry screen (Figure 11):

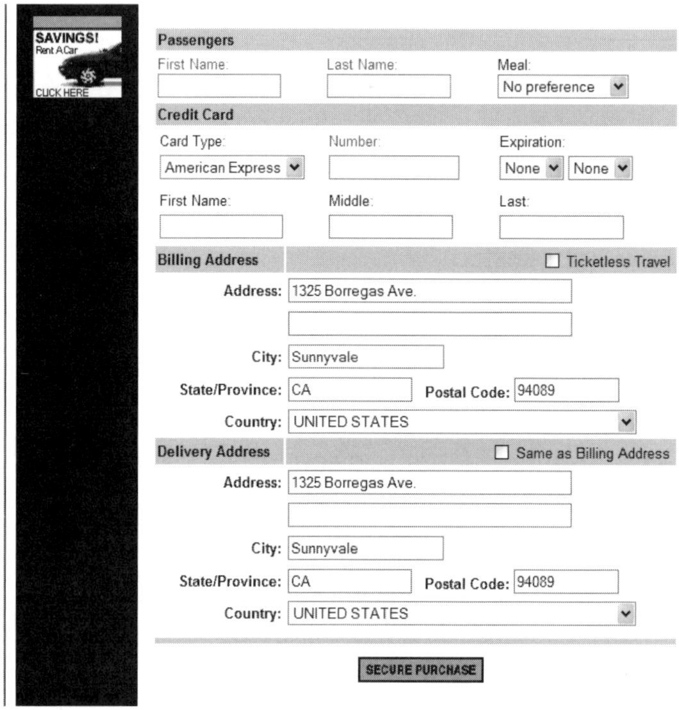

Figure 11: Flight booking

A test case for this business function, based on the specification, could look like this:

Flight number: **LH490**

Person flying:

- First name: **Andreas**
- Last name: **Golze**
- Meal: **No preference**

Credit card:

- Type: **VISA**
- Number: **1234567898**
- Expiration: **02 / 2010**
- Card holder:
  - First name: **Andreas**
  - Middle name:
  - Last name: **Golze**

Billing address:

- Street: **Fantasy Street**
- City: **Palo Alto**
- State: **CA**
- Postal Code: **12345**
- Country: **Somewhere**

Delivery address:

- **Same as billing address**

Expected result: **Flight will be successfully booked and the credit card will be billed.**

Before the test case can be executed with the data entry as defined, the data in the system has to be set up in such a way that the expected result will occur. First, we have to learn where the data is stored, so we need the data model for this business function. In most cases, talking to the developer will shorten this process.

Let's assume the data model looks like this (Figure 12):

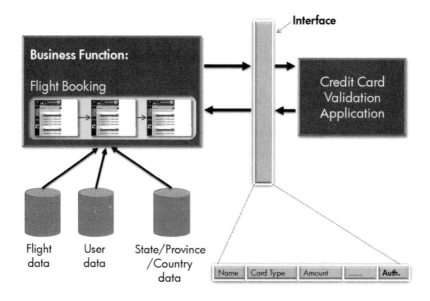

Figure 12: Flight booking interface and master data

Based on this information and the knowledge of the data we intend to use for the test case, we can now start setting up the master data.

Three fundamental strategies will all lead to a positive result:

- Take data from production
- Build data using the existing application
- Generate test data from scratch

Let's look at this in more detail.

Take Data from Production

The most common approach used in the industry is this: Save a copy of the data in production and load it into the test system. In our flight booking example, that would mean loading the existing customer database into the test environment.

The simplest way to get production data is to use the backup utilities that come with each system. A more sophisticated approach uses tools to "de-identify" the data before putting it into the test environment. Princeton Softech, an IBM company, is developing tools that can de-identify data for test environments.

Advantages of using production data:

- Implements easily

- Requires only storage space

- Works in every environment

- Involves no effort because it's already present and is only copied

- Represents production definitively, because it comes directly from the production environment

Disadvantages of using production data:

- De-identifying may involve a legal obligation, because of privacy restrictions

- Loads a huge amount of data, but you need only a very small portion

- Production status changes over time, so running regression tests is difficult without adjusting the test cases

This tempting approach is easy to apply, but it works in very few situations and should be a last-ditch method for obtaining test data. The biggest problem with this approach is that regression tests can't be performed without checking the data to see if it's still usable. So the effort saved in building the data is eaten up by the effort spent on each regression. Other negative factors include the time needed to reload the data, the waste of storage, and the big obstacles that need to be overcome when you try to automate.

We can see how this works (or doesn't) for our flight application: Over time, the flight tables change and suddenly a flight we used for one of our test cases no longer exists. So, if we're executing it automatically, the test will fail but not because of problems of the functionality, because of missing data.

This approach is still popular because most testing activities are conducted within a project framework where the maintenance costs that result from poor test data are not taken into account.

Build Data Using the Existing Application

In most cases, the best approach is to build the data you need using the existing application. Because applications are only very rarely built completely from scratch, there is nearly always an existing application to draw on. In our flight application example, we would enter our test flight plan into the system, build the test customer base, and go on with the protocol. We can use automated scripts for that, and whenever we do regression testing, we run the building scripts first.

We would use existing applications to generate customers, accounts, flights, and so forth. If automation tools are available, we can increase the efficiency.

Advantages:

- Generates the exact data required.
- Building the data can be automated.
- Regression tests can be automated.
- The environment can be kept small.
- Low data volume allows quick test environment setup and test evaluation.

Disadvantages:

- Data generation takes effort.
- Data may not completely represent the production-environment data.
- Interfaces may need to be simulated.

This approach is usually the most efficient way to obtain test data, especially when you're using tools for the data generation. Very often, the challenge is that testers need to have a full, complete, and consistent picture of the data involved. Because this information is not always available, it may take several iterations for the data environment to be complete and usable. But once the data environment is in place, the value is huge.

Generate Data from Scratch

This is the second best way to obtain test data. The idea is to build test data outside the real environment using the table definitions coming from the development team. This may be the only possible way to build test data in cases when the application is completely new.

This approach is also the only option when you're interface testing in early test phases and the real system is replaced by a simulator. For instance, if we want to test an order system that has an automated storage-area interface, we have to get data from the storage area for our test. The data can't come from real application usage, so we have to generate data and feed the interface using driver software.

Advantages:

- Generates the exact data we need.
- Regression tests can be automated.
- Environment can stay small.
- Low volume of data allows quick environment setup and test evaluation.

Disadvantages:

- Technical skills are required to build load routine, convert data, and build driver programs.
- Data may not completely represent production.
- Interfaces may need to be simulated.
- Tester is highly dependent on development information.

This approach is better than loading production data, but it requires a lot of technical knowledge and it is labor intensive. Some of the work can be eliminated if the development team builds the utilities so that they can be reused. The development team needs the load routines and the drivers for their development test (Unit Test) activities. Because the developers usually have no (or only limited) information about the data constellations in production, the work can be shared among teams: The test team provides the data and the development team comes up with the load routine and stubs.

To build the master data in our flight-booking example, we recommend a mix of the three techniques.

- Flight data and state/province/country data — take a copy from production. This data is fairly stable and we can save the effort necessary to build something new.

- User data — build with the application to enter new users to the system. With the list of users for our test cases, we build a Quick Test Professional script that generates users from the existing application.

- Interface — requires a *stub*, which is a program that stores data from our flight-booking application and gives back an authorization code as specified.

The best way to build this data is usually in Excel, where we put all the required data fields in columns and fill in a row for each test case. The information then goes into our test case description, so the tester knows what has to happen with the master data before he can execute the test.

Step 3: Finalize the Test Case Description

We've already built the core of the test case in the first two steps. The final step involves the environment and the aspects of test organization — the meta information — needed for the test execution and management of the whole process.

Let's start with the application itself. We need:

- Name and version of the application
- Test environment
- Information on testers, including special qualifications
- Execution date, execution time
- Link to test rule

Name and the version of the application. In a complex environment, several versions of the application may exist, and we have to use the correct version. If your organization has any configuration management, you can link the test case to the configured item. In an ideal process, the test case will be configured with the software version it was built for after successful completion.

Test Case Description No. 900			
Application under test			
Name			
Version		Test user	
Test environment		Password	

Test environment. Most companies have several environments available for test. The environment must be configured and set up in the correct way, so we specify which test environment we're using. In this situation, we need the name of the test user and a password. Test users simulate real users who are set up with certain rights, and we want the test to cover a real user situation.

Information on testers. To manage the test, we need information about those who will execute the test, so we can inform them and schedule the test. We also may need to mention special qualifications for testers.

Execution date, execution time. To organize the test, we need the execution date and, in some cases, the execution time. In a large test scenario, where hundreds of tests are executed on several consecutive days, it's important to know what was tested when.

Test Case Description No. 900			
Tester			
Name		**Execution date**	
Special qualification required			

Link to test rule. Finally, we link the test to the test rule, which is connected to a requirement. Linking these lets us show the test progress against the initial requirements.

Test Case Description No. 900	
Test rule covered	
Master data	

We have now closed the loop that started with structuring the requirements (Figure 13).

Figure 13: Requirements test loop

Test Scenarios

So far, we've covered the single test case. In most projects, or for most software products under test, we have to build up a test scenario over several days.

Here are some examples that illustrate this process:

Let's assume we want to test the "payment collection" business function. The payment collection process has several stages, starting with a reminder and ending with legal action. Let's assume the first three stages are handled by the system automatically.

Stage 1: After a bill is unpaid for 10 days, send a reminder letter.

Stage 2: After another 10 days, if the bill is not paid, send a warning letter with a handling fee of $10.

Stage 3: After another 10 days, if the bill is still not paid, send a pre-collection letter with a handling fee of $30.

The master data needed to test this function is unpaid bills of various values. The test execution requires a scenario where the system date changes for each test stage (Figure 14).

Test Case	Online day 1 (D)	Batch day 1(B)	Online Day 2 (d+10)	Batch Day 2 (B+10)	Online Day 3 (D+20)	Batch Day 3 (B+20)	Online Day 4 (D +30)	Batch Day 4 (B+30)
1	Enter Order	Generate bill Generate unpaid item		Send reminding letter Change status for unpaid item		Send dunning letter Change status of unpaid item		Send pre collection letter
2	Enter Order	Generate bill Generate unpaid item	Enter payment manually					
3	Enter Order	Generate bill Generate unpaid item		Process payment‡				

Figure 14: Test scenario plan for "payment collection"

To document the various test cases and the activities for test execution, we build a table for each business function. Before the test execution occurs, these tables are combined and the test scenario is built.

This usually happens in several iterations. The scenarios need to be as short as possible, which means the test is more efficient with fewer scenario days.

We also need to build the scenario in such a way that the data after each scenario day can be saved and reloaded at a later stage. This requires some planning because the date information is also stored. But if every scenario day can be reloaded at the tester's discretion, a regression test can be done pretty quickly. However, when the whole scenario has to be executed at once, the process is not as flexible and re-testing the application is more complicated. (In that case, automation may be an option, but the system date still has to be changed manually.)

Test Execution

When everything has been prepared we can start the execution of the test. The activities can be completely manual, completely automated, or (in most cases) a combination of automated and manual steps.

First we need a physical test environment and the correct version of the software to be tested. Note: We strongly recommend that a member of the test team install the software using the installation guidelines that come with the software, for two reasons:

- To ensure that the installation guidelines are correct and complete and that all elements of the software are there.

- To ensure that the installation is done in a defined-state test environment, and that test activities and other applications that should not be in the test environment during installation and test execution do not interfere.

A common mistake is to have the development team install the software and make last minute fixes if something goes wrong. If that's necessary, ask whether the software is ready for testing.

Second, we'll execute a *smoke test,* which is a small number of test cases that check the main functionalities. Be sure the development team knows that if one smoke test case fails, the software will be considered not ready for test. If you make the smoke test available to the development department, they can check it in their environment first before they hand the application over and you'll save time at the end. If the smoke test fails at that point, it is fair to assume that the installation or handover procedure is the problem and it can be fixed more quickly without lengthy discussions about who did what wrong.

Third, we'll load the master data and the test script into the environment (Figure 15).

Prepare the environment

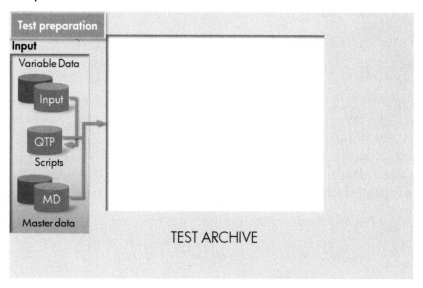

Figure 15: Test environment preparation

After all this is successful, the testers can begin the test execution (Figure 16). If test cases are automated, we can execute those first to gain confidence in the stability of the application.

Test execution

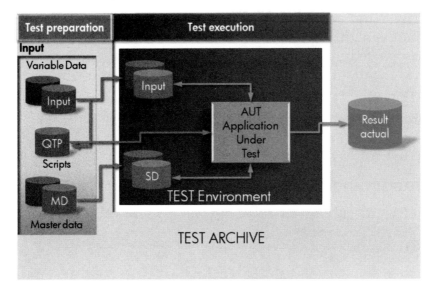

Figure 16: Test execution

We need to have access to the test environment only during the test execution. Test results are stored outside the test environment, so after the test execution is complete, the test results can be evaluated (Figure 17).

Test evaluation

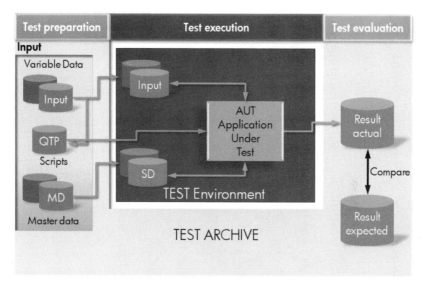

Figure 17: Test evaluation

To save time, we strongly recommend that you evaluate tests manually only if you find a lot of defects.

> A rule of thumb: As soon as more than 70 percent of the test cases can be executed without an issue, you can start automated test evaluation.

In automated test evaluation, we save the test results. After the next test cycle completes, the results are compared using utilities that show only the areas of concern. In other words, wherever the compare utility shows a difference in results, a defect has either been corrected or newly introduced, so the tester has to take action.

Step by step, the quality of the results should improve. At the end, we get a dataset that has 100 percent correct results that can be used as a reference for future tests.

Chapter 5

Test Optimization: Balancing Risk and Effort

In our view, testing is not just about finding defects and improving the quality of a product.

Test teams are never given enough time to perform all the rigors of testing, so they end up finding a balance between an acceptable defect rate and the investment necessary to get to that point. There are several ways to find that balance.

Our approach is always to take a business perspective and attempt to bridge the gap between business and IT. Because we believe that the business, with input from the testing team, should define the quality levels needed for a smooth operation, we've developed a test optimization approach called Business Impact Testing.

In this chapter, we'll explain how it works.

First, we analyze the business risk. Then, based on that risk, we can make specific decisions to optimize testing (Figure 18).

Optimize the Testing Effort

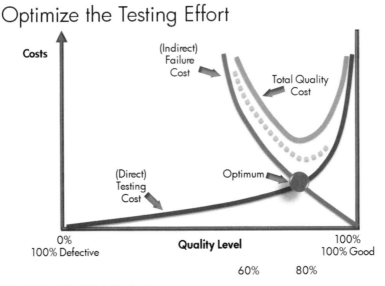

Source: J.M. Juran's Quality Control Handbook
Giga Information Group 2001, Justifying IT Investments: Quality Assurance

Figure 18: Diminishing returns of testing, finding the optimum point, and balancing risk and effort

The basic elements for our risk assessment are the business functions we obtain from the functional breakdown described in Chapter 2. We'll assess each of the business functions using a standardized approach.

The Business Impact Testing approach in the HP Software Quality Model follows these steps:

1. Assess the business impact of each business function.

2. Assess the probability of failure for each business function.

3. Derive the business risk from the result of these assessments.

4. Define the test procedure to apply for each risk level.

5. Assess the functional complexity of the business functions.

6. Calculate the effort for testing.

7. Balance the effort between automation and manual test execution based on the given parameters of your environment.

8. Adapt testing frameworks and leverage change impact to optimize testing effort.

Risk Assessment

In software, a risk threatens one or more of the functions the software is expected to perform and has an uncertain probability of occurring. We typically describe *risk* as a result of the probability that a failure will occur and the expected damage the failure can cause if it does occur.

Another way to see this is in this formula:

> Risk = damage caused by a failure X the probability the failure will happen

It's important to remember that the formula helps us understand the magnitude of the risk, but it does not help us cope with the uncertainty.

> We can calculate risk, but we can only estimate uncertainty. This exercise is more about comparison than accuracy.

Our approach uses this risk definition as a basis for our risk model. We built a model to assess risk in a very pragmatic way that requires only solid knowledge of the business and a good understanding of the system design. (We've seen some very complicated models that have not been successful in the field because they're too difficult to adopt and too technical. The learning curve of these risk models quickly increases the cost of testing and does not speak a business language.)

We want a risk model that's easy to understand and implement, but still gives us enough information to allow maximum test optimization.

Because our whole approach is about risk mitigation at a reasonable cost, we conduct the risk assessment to achieve the following goals:

- Transparency of the functionality under test
- Focus on business-critical functions
- Knowledge of the test coverage

If we use the result of the functional breakdown and assess each business function, we'll achieve those goals.

We assign the functionality with the highest business risk the highest priority, and we determine the effort to expend and which test activities to undertake for a single business function based on the prioritization of risk.

> To calculate business risk, we need to determine the damage we would expect from a failure and the probability of the failure to occur.

As a result, we conduct our risk assessment in two phases.

First, we assess the impact to the business of each business function. *Impact* in this context means to what extent we need the functionality in order to perform the business' day-to-day operations, or how much damage a failure of the function will cause to the business.

Second, we look at the probability that a defect will occur in the assessed business function.

After we have completed these two steps, we'll derive the risk for each business function as a result of both values.

Business Impact Analysis

First, we conduct the business impact analysis for all business functions that belong to the application under test. We use criteria that are common for all business units so the results are comparable throughout the enterprise.

Business impact criteria are defined in terms of the damage to the business if a failure were to occur (Figure 19).

Criteria	Result		
	a High Impact	b Medium Impact	c Low Impact
Type of process	Calculation / validation	Change of data	Display
Business implication	Legal	Wrong information	None
Frequency of use	Very often	Often	Rare
Number of customers affected	Large number / very important	Group	Some

Figure 19: Sample business impact analysis

We've based this information on many successful implementations where it has proven sufficient and practical. We can change or adapt the criteria of course, depending on the individual situation in a given environment.

During the assessment, we check each business function against each criterion. The result of the analysis allows us to categorize all the business functions into three business impact categories: high, medium, and low.

We determine the impact using a formula agreed upon by the business and testing team.

For the example in Figure 19, we might use the following formula:

- **High impact** — Any business function with two or more high-impact criteria; or two or more medium-impact criteria and one criteria with high impact.

- **Medium impact** — Any business function with two or more medium-impact criteria and none with high impact; or one high-impact criteria, one with medium impact, and all other criteria with low impact.

- **Low impact** — Any other combinations.

This is, of course, just an example and we would modify this formula for different situations.

Note: In HP Quality Center 9.2 and higher, the entire business risk analysis has been automated. For more information, contact an HP representative.

Failure Probability

Like the business impact, the failure probability is the result of an assessment based on criteria that should be standard for the whole company (Figure 20).

Criteria	Result		
	III Unlikely	II Likely	I Very Likely
Change rate	Unchanged	Changed function	New function
Software maturity	Mature (> 10 years)	Progressing (5 -10 years)	Immature (< 5 years)
Defect rate	Low	Medium	High

Figure 20: Failure probability

Depending on a given environment, we can change and adapt the criteria.

During the assessment, each business function is checked with each criterion. Again, we can categorize business functions into three probability categories: very likely, likely, and unlikely.

We determine the impact from an agreed upon formula. Using the example in the table above, we suggest applying the following formula:

- **Very likely** — Any business function with two or more criteria that are very likely to occur; or two or more criteria that are likely and one criterion that is very likely to occur.

- **Likely** — Any business function with two or more criteria likely to occur and none that is very likely to occur; or one criteria very likely to occur, one likely to occur, and all other criteria being unlikely to occur.

- **Unlikely** — Any other combinations.

After we have completed the assessment and have a value for the impact and the probability, we make the final step to derive the final business risk.

Derive Business Risk

We calculate the risk based on the combined results of the business impact analysis and the failure probability assessment. The combination allows us to finally categorize the business functions in terms of high risk, medium risk, or low risk (Figure 21).

Impact	Probability		
	III Unlikely	II Likely	I Very Likely
a High impact	Medium risk	High risk	High risk
b Medium impact	Low risk	Medium risk	Medium risk
c Low impact	Low risk	Low risk	Medium risk

Figure 21: Calculating risk categories

After we've calculated the risk, we can design the test procedure to be applied during Integration testing for the business function.

Test Procedure Definition

We define different test procedures for each risk level with the risk analysis information.

> **The key is to invest testing resources corresponding to the risk level.**

A test procedure lays out the test strategy we'll apply to:

- Define the test approach.

- Select the test data.

- Set the test optimization level (using automation, business process frameworks, or other test strategies).

We typically devise an effective test procedure from a combination of experience and mathematical calculations. To keep things simple for now, we only show the test procedure example based on our experiences (Figure 22). (We'll discuss how to determine the optimum mix between automation and manual testing later in this chapter.)

Test Procedures Approach Based on Risk		
High risk	Procedure	Systematic testing using equivalence partitioning with combinations, and root-cause analysis
	Approach	Automate 30% with Business Process testing framework, manual test 70%, leverage change
Medium risk	Procedure	Systematic testing with or without using equivalence partitioning without combinations, and root-cause analysis
	Approach	Use traditional automation 20%, manual 80%
Low risk	Procedure	Systematic or ad hoc testing
	Approach	Automated: 5% Manual: 95%, outsource testing

Figure 22: Sample test procedures

Adapt the test procedure to the specific needs of the business the application is written for.

Functional Complexity

Next, we assess the functional complexity of each business function to estimate the effort we should budget for the testing activities.

> Being able to estimate testing efforts allows us to better plan the software testing lifecycle, align resources, and leverage test strategies and technology.

We know that functions involving a large number of assets, such as data sets, interfaces, or components, take more time to test than a function that involves only a few assets. Each test requires preliminary activities, such as test case development, data preparation, and test result evaluation.

After we complete the risk assessment and define the test procedure for each risk class, we've laid the foundation to estimate the test effort. But we need to know the functional complexity of the business function.

Functional complexity analysis indicates the amount of testing development effort we expect to go into the business function. More complex requirements lead to a more complex implementation that is more error prone and thus needs more testing.

From a testing point of view, the functional complexity depends on the number of objects or assets involved in the business function. Objects, in this case, do not refer to an object-oriented approach, but rather to all kinds of assets, such as tables, data sets, forms, and templates. The tester has to prepare and evaluate the data for each such object (Figure 23).

Criteria	Result		
	1 High Complexity	2 Medium Complexity	3 Low Complexity
Number of objects affected	>9	4-9	<4
Number of objects with write access	>3	1-3	<1
Number of objects with read access	>5	3-5	<3
Number of windows affected	>4	2-4	<2

Figure 23: Functional complexity

As in the risk assessment, we'll assess all business functions against each criterion. We'll derive the results using the following rules:

- **Risk class 1** — A business function rated 1 at least twice; or 1 once and 2 at least twice.

- **Risk class 2** — A business function rated 2 at least twice; or 1 once and 2 once.

- **Risk class 3** — All other cases.

Test Effort Estimation

Starting with the effort each business function requires, and depending on the test procedure we've defined and the functional complexity, we can make test effort estimations.

Based on many projects, we've built a test effort baseline model that organizations can use when its own numbers are not available.

The following matrix shows the effort that has to be spent in Integration testing to execute the respective test procedures. (The numbers come from projects delivered in the past five years.)

Test Effort for Integration Test
Not Optimized

	1 High Complexity	2 Medium Complexity	3 Low Complexity	Test Procedure
A High Risk	13 - 19	10 – 16	7- 13	Procedure for high risk
B Medium Risk	6.5 – 9.5	6.5 – 9.5	4 – 6.5	Procedure for medium risk
C Low Risk	2.3	2.2	1.2 – 2.2	Procedure for low risk

Effort in person-days for test case development, test data definition, test script development, test execution, and test evaluation per business function

To get a better understanding of how much work goes into which activity, we have broken down the overall effort into the different activities:

1. Develop test cases for the high- and medium-risk business functions, using the behavioral modeling described in Chapter 3.

Test Case Development Effort

	1 High Complexity	2 Medium Complexity	3 Low Complexity	Test Procedure
A **High Risk**	4 - 6	3 – 5	2- 4	Procedure for high risk
B **Medium Risk**	2 - 3	2 - 3	1 – 2	Procedure for medium risk
C **Low Risk**	1	1	0.5 - 1	Procedure for low risk

Effort in person-days for test case development per business function

2. Develop or define the test data by completing two tasks.

   First, we have to define the test data that goes into the test rule. Second, we have to define the test data that must be in the system to serve as the data environment for the test case. For example, if the test case is about to close an account, this account has to be in the system and open to make sure the test case leads to a positive result.

Test Data Development Effort

	1 High Complexity	2 Medium Complexity	3 Low Complexity	Test Procedure
A **High Risk**	4 - 6	3 – 5	2- 4	Procedure for high risk
B **Medium Risk**	2 - 3	2 - 3	1 – 2	Procedure for medium risk
C **Low Risk**	1	1	0.5 - 1	Procedure for low risk

Effort in person-days for test data development per
business function

3. Create the test scripts for automation. We start with a fairly low amount of test automation, like 30 percent for high-risk business functions and 20 percent for medium-risk business functions. But even this low amount of automation takes some effort.

Test Script Development Effort

	1 High Complexity	2 Medium Complexity	3 Low Complexity	Test Procedure
A High Risk	2 - 3	1 – 2	1- 2	Procedure for high risk
B Medium Risk	1	1	0.5 - 1	Procedure for medium risk
C Low Risk	n.a.	n.a.	n.a.	Procedure for low risk

Effort in person-days for test script development per business function

4. Apply the test evaluation effort only for the test cases we're automating — for manual test cases, the evaluation takes place during the execution.

Test Evaluation Effort

	1 High Complexity	2 Medium Complexity	3 Low Complexity	Test Procedure
A High Risk	2 - 3	2 - 3	1 - 2	Procedure for high risk
B Medium Risk	1 - 2	1 - 2	1	Procedure for medium risk
C Low Risk	0	0	0	Procedure for low risk

Effort in person-days for test evaluation per business function

5. Estimate the effort for one manual test execution. Each test case, whether or not it will be automated, is usually executed at least once manually as a best practice.

Manual Test Execution Effort

	1 High Complexity	2 Medium Complexity	3 Low Complexity	Test Procedure
A High Risk	1	1	1	Procedure for high risk
B Medium Risk	0.5	0.5	0.5	Procedure for medium risk
C Low Risk	0.3	0.2	0.2	Procedure for low risk

Effort in person-days for manual test execution per business function

By taking the business-impact approach, we make sure to concentrate the test activities on the most critical business functions.

How to Calculate the Optimal Level of Automation

Examining the effort for the different activities inevitably brings up the question of what level of test automation is the optimum from a cost-value ratio.

Using the same sample scenario from above, we compare the additional effort required for automation to a single complete manual test cycle per risk class.

Additional Effort for Automation

	1 High Complexity	2 Medium Complexity	3 Low Complexity	Test Procedure
A **High Risk**	1.5 − 2.5	0.5 − 1.5	0.5 − 1.5	Procedure for high risk
B **Medium Risk**	0.25	0.25	0 − 0.25	Procedure for medium risk
C **Low Risk**	0	0	0	Procedure for low risk

Additional effort in person-days for test automation
compared to manual test execution per business function

This chart represents the extra effort or investment required for automation compared to a complete manual test.

In the next chart, which shows the second step, we're looking at the savings we achieve through automation for each test cycle after the initial investment of effort to automate the test.

Effort Saved through Automation

	1 High Complexity	2 Medium Complexity	3 Low Complexity	Test Procedure
A **High Risk**	0.5	0.5	0.5	Procedure for high risk
B **Medium Risk**	0.25	0.25	0.25	Procedure for medium risk
C **Low Risk**	0	0	0	Procedure for low risk

Effort in person-days for one test cycle per business
function

The calculated savings over time would allow automated tests to break even with manual tests after a few test cycles, depending on test automation level.

Number of Cycles Needed to Break Even

	1 High Complexity	2 Medium Complexity	3 Low Complexity	Test Procedure
A **High Risk**	3 - 5	1 - 3	1 − 3	Procedure for high risk
B **Medium Risk**	1	1	0 − 1	Procedure for medium risk
C **Low Risk**	0	0	0	Procedure for low risk

Additional effort in person-days for test automation
compared to manual test execution per business function

The higher the complexity and risk, the more cycles are needed in order to break even.

Now, let's look at the same figures with a higher percentage of automation. We're assuming that we automate all test cases.

The additional effort would be as shown in the next chart.

Additional Effort for Automation

	1 High Complexity	2 Medium Complexity	3 Low Complexity	Test Procedure
A **High Risk**	5.5 – 8.5	1.5 – 5.5	1.5 – 5.5	100% automation
B **Medium Risk**	2.25	2.25	1- 2.25	100% automation
C **Low Risk**	0	0	0	Manual

Additional effort in person-days for test automation
compared to manual test execution per business function

Based on those figures, the savings for each test cycle after the initial test cycle is shown in the next chart.

Effort Saved through Automation

	1 High Complexity	2 Medium Complexity	3 Low Complexity	Test Procedure
A **High Risk**	1.5	1.5	1.5	100% automation
B **Medium Risk**	0.75	0.75	0.75	100% automation
C **Low Risk**	0	0	0	Procedure for low risk

Effort in person-days for one test cycle per
business function

This leads to the following number of test cycles that would allow us to break even.

Number of Cycles Needed to Break Even

	1 High Complexity	2 Medium Complexity	3 Low Complexity	Test Procedure
A High Risk	3 - 5	1 - 3	1 – 3	100% automation
B Medium Risk	2 - 3	2 - 3	1 - 3	100% automation
C Low Risk	0	0	0	Procedure for low risk

Additional effort in person-days for test automation
compared to manual test execution per business function

Looking at the total picture, it becomes clear that the number of cycles needed to break even goes up, and we assume it's possible to handle the challenges with the test data.

Remember that these sample numbers are a best-case scenario, assuming we're following the proper Business Impact Testing strategies, using the best traditional automation solutions, and employing expert test automation engineers.

In most organizations, the test cycles required for test automation to break even with manual testing can be much higher. It's very important to do these calculations for your specific environment to get to your optimum test automation levels. Generally, 30 to 50 percent test automation has proven to be the optimum level for most situations using traditional test automation techniques. In the next section, we introduce a couple of new concepts that can significantly improve the return on investment and efficiencies of test automation.

Test Effort Optimization

Looking at the different activities that need to be performed to a complete testing, we've isolated some areas where efficiency can be improved.

Improving Test Automation and Manual Testing

The following points describe why test automation can increase an organization's testing efficiencies; however, the extra investment and existing organizational skill sets often make this adoption slow. To make test automation feasible, we need to combine traditional technological approaches with business-oriented testing frameworks.

- Automation can drastically reduce the effort needed for regression testing.

- Automation can enable last-minute sanity checks during fast-change cycles when it's impossible to test manually because of time constraints.

- Automation enables consistency and logic coverage. There is no risk that test cases are left out or errors are overlooked if they are designed correctly.

- Automation gives the option for a higher regression rate because only computing time is involved when running the test.

To achieve these improvements, we can leverage a combination of new testing frameworks and new testing technologies. Let's examine a couple of the most interesting and profound of these improvements.

Over the past years, several improvements have made testing more efficient, and the latest comes from the Business Process testing framework (Figure 24).

Evolution of Testing

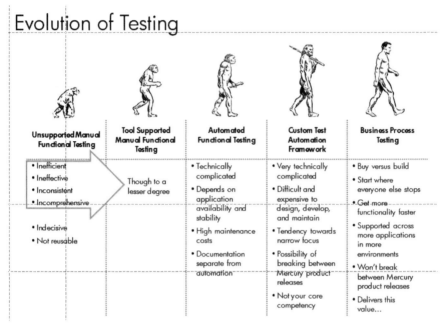

Unsupported Manual Functional Testing	Tool Supported Manual Functional Testing	Automated Functional Testing	Custom Test Automation Framework	Business Process Testing
• Inefficient • Ineffective • Inconsistent • Incomprehensive • Indecisive • Not reusable	Though to a lesser degree	• Technically complicated • Depends on application availability and stability • High maintenance costs • Documentation separate from automation	• Very technically complicated • Difficult and expensive to design, develop, and maintain • Tendency towards narrow focus • Possibility of breaking between Mercury product releases • Not your core competency	• Buy versus build • Start where everyone else stops • Get more functionality faster • Supported across more applications in more environments • Won't break between Mercury product releases • Delivers this value...

Figure 24: Five generations of testing improvements

HP Business Process Testing software is one of the most profound and revolutionary new test frameworks for optimizing testing today. But to fully understand the benefits and appreciate the value of this approach, we must first understand the history of software testing over the past 15 to 20 years.

Manual testing was originally the only method of software testing. A lead tester would typically design the test cases and, if you were lucky, you got a printed sheet of paper with instructions on how to navigate the software and hints about the results you should expect to see when you navigated the software.

Testing was mostly ad hoc and inconsistent, and test coverage was poor.

Automated software testing was invented to address these issues. Although the concept of automated software testing has been around for quite some time, it's still being adopted only reluctantly in many organizations. As a matter of fact, based on what we see in the industry, about 80 percent of software applications are still tested manually.

Automated software testing advancements have come a long way in a short time. Each successive generation of solutions has handled more significant challenges, yet each advance has introduced a new set of issues to be resolved.

First-generation products, introduced about 15 years ago, were hardware-based capture/playback systems, like macros that recorded keystrokes and replayed them on demand. These tests were easy to create, but they had limited validations and checkpoints, and they were difficult to maintain and document as changes occurred.

Second-generation solutions, appearing about 10 years ago, were software-based capture/playback systems that recorded test cases and represented them as scripts. This approach gave us wider test coverage and more robust checkpoints and validations, but required specialized development skills and did not completely solve the maintenance challenge. Every time an application changed, the test scripts had to be updated, which meant modifications to many lines of code and continual documentation updates to reflect these changes.

Third-generation automated testing solutions, called "test frameworks," have been on the market since 2001. Test frameworks added a layer of abstraction over the scripting process so non-technical people could build tests.

With this approach, subject matter experts (SMEs or business analysts) could draw on a library of prebuilt "keywords," which implemented a specific action against the application (for example, "click the OK button"). Keywords made it possible to develop automated test cases with no procedural programming experience.

Test frameworks led to dramatic productivity increases for many software testing teams, but they still had many shortcomings. For example:

- The operations performed by any particular keyword tended to be very fine-grained or atomic. Designing a test for an entire business process required hundreds of individual keywords, which is a time-consuming process.

- Because test framework solutions consist of files with keywords and their associated data elements, SMEs found they were still creating scripts, despite promises of "scriptless test design."

- Traditional test framework products were not always backward compatible with previous-generation technology (such as recorders), which limited their flexibility and power. Test engineers couldn't get under the hood and modify the code underlying the keywords even if they wanted to.

- Test frameworks and keyword-based products still didn't function at the business process level, which forced SMEs to think like programmers and constrained adoption rates.

- Test frameworks did not help create test documentation, and therefore many man-hours were needed to assemble the detailed information required for compliance with several legislative acts that regulate data access, including Sarbanes Oxley and the Health Information Portability and Accountability Act (HIPAA).

It was clear that a simple modification or enhancement to previous generation software testing solutions would continue to solve some problems, but cause others.

We needed a revolutionary approach that could radically streamline test design, test automation, test maintenance, and the expensive and time-consuming test documentation processes. The latest generation of testing solutions was built on the experiences of the previous 15 years.

> **HP Business Process Testing is the first complete role-based test framework to bridge the quality chasm by enabling business analysts and quality engineers to collaborate effectively.**

The HP Business Process Testing framework enables non-technical SMEs to build, data-drive, execute, and document test steps without deep technical knowledge. They can create high-level test flows that mirror actual business processes, which frees quality engineers to concentrate their efforts on areas that facilitate automation.

The benefits of HP Business Process Testing far surpass any of the previous generation of testing solutions:

- It greatly simplifies and speeds up the test-design process by using components (business-process building blocks) (Figure 25).

- It allows QA and testing teams to start the test-design process much sooner — during system design — which accelerates time to deployment for high-quality software.

- It generates automated tests and test-case documentation in a *single step,* which eliminates the expensive and time-consuming processes of creating and maintaining test records.

- It enables QA teams to use prepackaged test assets and best practices to implement test automation for leading enterprise resource planning (ERP) and customer relationship manager (CRM) applications, which saves time and leverages the knowledge of experts.

- It raises the adoption rate for test automation because it's so easy to deploy and use.

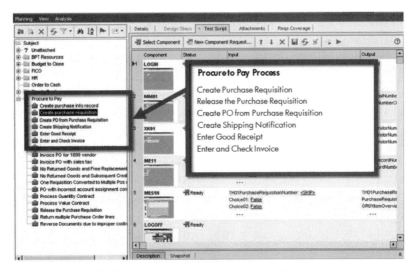

Figure 25: Examples of components and business processes

To demonstrate the advantages of Business Process testing, let's look at the flight-booking application from Chapter 2. In that case, the process that needs to be tested would look like Figure 26.

Business Process (example)

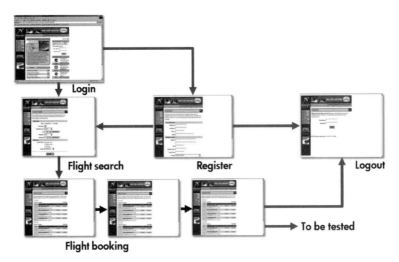

Figure 26: Sample business process for a flight application

Let's now assume that a small change in the LOGIN business function introduces two new fields, because we'll integrate a new business process (Figure 27).

Business Process (new)

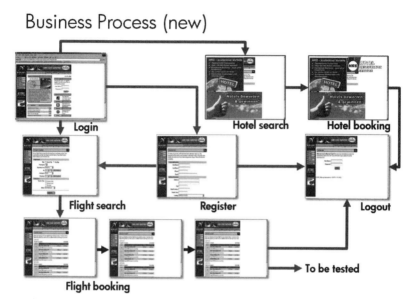

Figure 27: Sample flight application with new business process

In the old days, all the scripts using LOGIN would have to be adapted, which is a major rework effort. With HP Business Process Testing, the change only has to take place in one component and after that, the whole automation works again.

Hence HP Business Process Testing lays the foundation for successful test automation with increased efficiencies and acceptable maintenance effort.

In an ideal world, we could generate the test automation based on the specification, or better yet, the requirement. But, in the real world, we always recommend that you run the test at least once manually before you automate to verify that the test case properly covers the requirements.

The advantage of using HP Business Process Testing is that it is a framework that works for both manual and automated testing. It allows us to design test components as early as the requirements-definition phase, before the business function is fully programmed or developed.

This means we can start testing much earlier, but it also means that we can now align the design of the test components much more closely with the business requirements.

Also, we no longer have to follow the old two-step process of creating manual test cases — verify them once and then create automated tests. With HP Business Process Testing, this is a one-step process (Figure 28).

> Using the Business Process Testing framework to enhance the traditional test automation technologies and concepts allows us to achieve a better software quality level with the same quality investment.

Automation as Part of the Strategy

Source: J.M. Juran's Quality Control Handbook
Giga Information Group 2001, Justifying IT Investments: Quality Assurance

Figure 28: Automation and test frameworks allow higher quality level at a lower total cost

Improving Regression Test Efficiency

Although many organizations now pay more attention to quality process and testing efficiencies for new applications or projects, testing processes for patches, minor releases, and upgrades are generally poor. There are several reasons for this.

Most new implementations involve a large staff, with a budget for enough time and resources. After an application goes live, only a small team of developers and testers are kept to maintain the system. Given that almost every change to a production system is deemed critical, the already reduced testing team never has enough time to run through the proper regression tests.

The increased complexity of today's applications only adds to the problem — every patch to a system possibly impacts dozens of others.

Test planning becomes a very difficult task. Testing teams faced with these challenges can:

- Ask for enough time to run through a full 100 percent regression to ensure all bases are covered.

- Test only the changed component and hope it has no impact on other areas of the application.

- Not test changes at all and cross their fingers.

- Convince management to reject the changes (which hardly ever happens).

Regardless of what they decide, risk is either significantly increased from not testing enough or effort is wasted if a full 100 percent regression is run for every change.

Change impact testing is gaining a lot of traction. The new technology aims to perform a change-impact analysis for every patch or minor release, and then determine exactly which application modules are impacted and which test cases must be regression tested.

So instead of having to run a full regression, we only need to test a small percentage of the regression tests that cover the impacted modules of the application. This solution assures that we can release applications with the highest quality at the lowest level of risk (Figure 29).

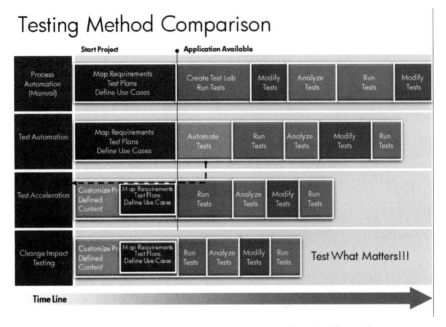

Figure 29: Change impact testing can drastically reduce the testing effort

So far in this book, we have discussed testing strategies and concepts that, when leveraged properly, can help drastically improve testing efficiencies and cost effectiveness.

We can implement each separately or together to gain the most benefits. No matter how many techniques you implement or ways you optimize testing, you won't really know if it has improved your software quality unless you can measure, analyze, and compare your testing efforts and software quality over time.

In the next chapter, we discuss our *SUCCESSFUL* goal-driven approach to measuring.

Chapter 6

Why Bother with Non-Functional Testing?

Most of this book covers functional test activities. Non-functional testing checks to make sure a system can deliver in a broader context. How does it perform if some part of the system fails? What is its capacity under an increased load?

For instance, we all know computers can crash and that core business processes are handled by IT. Yet, often very little effort is spent learning how the system behaves in case of a system failure.

> It's critical to make sure that a disk crash does not result in severe business disruption.

Companies tend to focus on functional testing and often only perform non-functional tests late in the process, when development is close to deadline. Little time remains to overcome problems that surface at this phase, and if a test fails, the whole project could topple.

Because we usually believe that all components must function before we start non-functional tests, these are carried out at the end of development. Nevertheless, the non-functional

requirements are considered at the conception time: architecture and design will take into consideration that the system is
robust and can operate despite a disk failure. Hence, non-functional testing has to start by validating that the requirements
are well addressed by architecture and design, before starting
the development.

> All components have to function before we can
> look at the non-functional aspects.

Testing an automobile is a good illustration of this reasoning. If
a car is not completely assembled, you can't conduct a speed
test or a crash test. However, if you have the quality goals that
lead to these test phases in mind early, you can plan for the
tests. And it's best to do as many early tests as possible.

Car manufacturers are considering crash performance early in
the process. They make sure that safety belts are well posi-
tioned and are fixed to strong points of the car. This is
addressed at the design stage, as well as being validated before
production starts.

How, then, do we integrate thorough non-functional testing
into our project? How is non-functional testing different from
functional testing, and how do we carry it out?

Non-Functional Scope

Non-functional testing covers all the elements of a solution not
directly related to the business process, but key to operating
the solution.

What happens in the application environment — and the
events that occur during the test — are more important than
the test result itself. Non-functional testing analyzes what happens during the test. Even when the test is successful, check
why it is successful — that information will be useful for operations.

The elements we usually consider are (Figure 30):

- Performance
- Load
- Availability
- Reliability

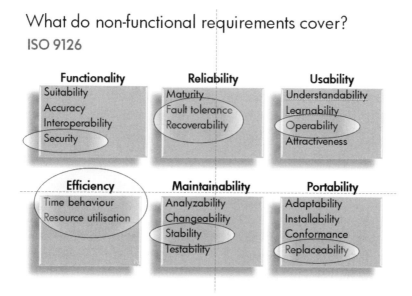

Figure 30: Non-functional requirements scope (ISO 9126)

Performance

Performance testing involves the execution speed of the system. This activity has one goal, to reach the required performance level. Make sure enough information is captured during the test to help identify why the expected performance is, or is not, reached.

Load

Performance testing and load testing are often confused. Load testing involves the usage level an application can sustain and performance testing is about execution speed. So load testing verifies whether the expected load can be sustained. In this stage, we consider why the load is supported or not supported, and what should be done to reach the required level.

Availability

Here we test whether a given system can deliver its services even if expected or unexpected events occur. Typically, you'll determine if you can deliver services while you're performing expected activities, such as rolling out a new application release or performing backup.

But we also consider unforeseen events. Availability testing may mean finding out if the service still delivers when a disk crashes, the network is down, or the CPU is not functioning. Availability testing can look at disaster recovery, demonstrating that even a flood, fire, power failure, or earthquake doesn't result in a major service disruption.

Reliability

This ultimate phase of non-functional testing evaluates the consequences of unexpected failures (software or hardware) during problematic execution steps -- disk failure in the middle of a transaction, a database crash during a write execution, or memory failure during processing. This kind of activity is also called "destructive testing" because it involves stress to the system.

We're demonstrating that, even in very difficult circumstances, the system remains coherent. So reliability testing is not done just to prove that the system still operates under such circumstances, but also to show that even when something impossible happens (like all backup systems fail at the same time), system coherency is preserved: When you restart it, the service will begin where it stopped, or from a defined point, without major business data loss.

Figure 31 illustrates a non-functional testing sequence.

Figure 31: Non-functional testing sequence

Consider Non-Functional Testing at the Business Level

Some see non-functional requirements as technical issues that have little to do with business requirements — after all, the testing is usually performed late in the development lifecycle. But that perspective is a mistake.

> Non-functional requirements are really business requirements.

The following dialogue is an example of how to turn the technical description into a description of business requirements through a series of questions and answers:

Q: How many simultaneous connections must the system support?

A: 10,000

Q: What do we do with connection 10,001? Reject it, or downgrade performance slightly by 0.01%?

A: Downgrade performances up to 1% evenly.

Q: So, we can handle up to 11,000 simultaneous connections; what do we do with connection 11,001?

A: Reject.

Q: Even if it's a VIP?

A: No, cut one non-priority connection.

At the end of such a discussion, the test cases become obvious.

> The first stage of non-functional testing is to turn non-functional requirements into business requirements.

Start with the architecture phase of the lifecycle — we know a poor architecture means bad performance. Senior architects can review the architecture to detect flaws that should be fixed before design — it's how you start fixing bugs before development begins.

> The second step in non-functional testing is to validate the architecture to make sure it can deliver the non-functional requirements.

As with functional testing, we establish a test lifecycle for the non-functional tests. Conducting tests at the earliest stage of the lifecycle saves time, effort, and money. The cost curve below shows that potential damage from non-functional elements can be significantly higher than that from functional issues.

Figure 32 outlines the steps to perform non-functional testing.

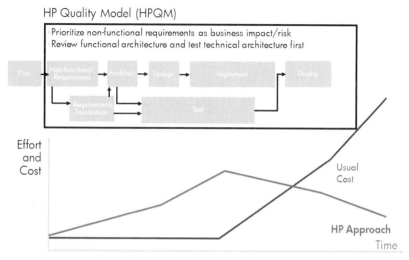

Figure 32: HP non-functional testing methodology

Non-functional testing in various lifecycle stages often shows the need for architectural changes. These changes have different impacts depending on when they are considered. Table 2 shows potential consequences related to the state at which architectural changes are considered.

Stage	Possible Changes
After design completion	■ Change design. ■ Delay development and testing.
After or during development	■ Change design or continue with an inadequate design because of cost to change. ■ Implement ad hoc fixes. ■ Increase maintenance and operation costs. ■ Halt project.

Table 2: Possible affects of changes at different stages

Stage	Possible Changes
After deployment	■ Assess business impact. ■ Accept operational workaround and trade-offs for functionality. ■ Operate business at higher cost and greater risk. ■ Lose reputation or market share as result of business impact.

Table 2: Possible affects of changes at different stages (continued)

Performance Testing

During performance testing, we check whether the system is executing in a defined time, and characteristic business processes can be test cases. The result of the test is not as important as what you can observe during the test execution.

Divide performance testing into these six steps (Figure 33):

1. Performance requirements definition
2. Performance breakdown
3. Performance instrumentation
4. Performance test execution
5. Performance test analysis
6. Performance enhancements

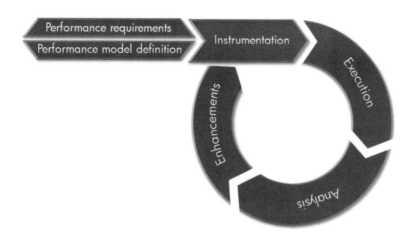

Figure 33: Performance testing cycle

Step 1: Defining Performance Requirements

We usually express the performance requirement as the time elapsed between the user action and the result display — all the steps that analyze user input and data presentation.

For fully automated tasks, or batches, consider the speed between the launch time and the end of the job. When a process involves data displayed for end users on a screen, the time calculation takes display time into consideration.

> Performance is the elapsed time between two well-defined steps of the process.

It's important to define performance requirements as business requirements by considering key business processes and defining the maximum execution time for each.

> The execution time (ET) depends on the system load (L) and can be expressed as a mathematical function (f).
>
> $$ET = f(L)$$

The technical platform will define the function, but we also have to see how the function performs in a given environment. For the sake of demonstration, we assume the performance requirements specify that the process between the user request and display of results should not take more than 7 seconds.

Step 2: Performance Breakdown

After the performance requirements have been defined, the next step is to break down the business processes of the test cases into the smallest possible steps. The goal is to:

- Identify which steps the application development team controls, and what is beyond your control (for instance, use of a third-party network).
- Define the execution speed of each step.
- Define focal points.
- Build the performance testing strategy and plan.

To understand the steps of a business process, consider a standard web application where an end user uses a browser to access an ordering system (Figure 34).

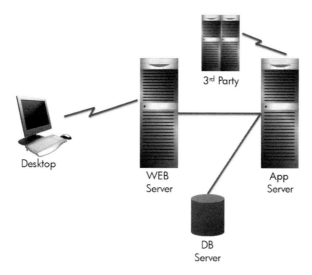

Figure 34: Web application architecture example

End users can browse a catalog, download item details to browse off-line, and place orders online.

The performance breakdown has to identify all the elements of the architecture and separate the whole process into independent components. Performance requirements will then be refined to time spent in each step at each component level. The performance breakdown in that case will consider:

- Execution on the desktop
- Communication between the desktop and the web server
- Web server
- Web container
- Communication with the application server
- EJBs execution
- Third interaction
- Database access
- Database queries execution

This breakdown allows you to build the system-performance model, which is a key element for performance testing.

Evaluate performance requirements for each sub-element from what's expected on the global market. Initially, assign each element in the list a percentage of the time the whole transaction should take. In our example, we assign 30% for the database-query execution. This process is based on experience or on the data collected during performance analysis.

Step	Percentage	Absolute Value (seconds)
1. Execution on the desktop	5%	0.35
2. Communication between desktop and web server	3%	0.21
3. Web server	0.5%	0.035
4. Web container	0.5%	0.035
5. Communication with application server	1%	0.07
6. EJBs execution	20%	1.4
7. External systems interaction	35%	2.45
8. Transaction management / database access	5%	0.35
9. Database queries execution	30%	2.1

Table 3: High-level performance model

The values in the table reflect the time each single step should take. But it depends on the load (the number of simultaneous users) the system can support on the various parts. Let's have a look.

Step 3: Performance Instrumentation

After you've defined the performance of individual elements and set up the objectives, capture the information with tools and code that track the time spent in the various parts of the application. It's what we call "instrumentation." Keep in mind:

- Instrumentation should not alter the normal method of executing the application, so it should not alter the time spent.

- The measure has to be accurate, so you should know what you're measuring.

The first point depends on the context: At the upper-application level, performance measures have almost no impact. When the problems are fine-grained and require a lot of measures to be taken, latency may add processing time that will alter the results. The impact will be a problem when performances are evaluated under load stress (see "Load Testing" on page 128). To limit the impact, use a "dichotomical" approach (see next section).

The second point can be harder to achieve: At a high level, you may want to capture the time spent in executing one big chunk of the application. For example, in an order-management system you might measure the time spent between submission of order data and the return of a successful operation to the user. The value for this execution time includes unforeseen elements:

- The operating system may interrupt your application execution, leading to latency in the execution.

- If you use a virtual machine, control the element that will impact execution of your application, along with the obvious garbage collection.

- External libraries execute code outside your control.

- The first time you access data from files or databases, it must be read on the disc, loaded into memory, and eventually cached; when you access the data later, it will take less time.

When performance really matters, all the details must be analyzed and documented. For example, the time spent during the first data access gives information on the time needed to launch the system.

Step 4: Performance Test Execution

After performance tests have been specified and the performance measurement is in place, performance testing can start.

The first test is a platform validation to make sure the configuration defined in the previous step has been set up correctly. System test tools (such as CPU consumption meters, memory usage, disk access, network throughput, and I/O controls) must be up and running at this point to allow graphical real-time visualization of these parameters.

It's important to look to these indicators during test execution — they'll show at a glance if something is going significantly wrong during the test execution. Usually, the biggest problems occur during the first tests. But the initial test usually shows mistakes that can be easily fixed and bring significant improvement. It's common to see systems that are 10 times slower than expected in the initial test phase.

Step 5: Performance Test Analysis

After you've completed the performance tests, go through the resulting data to evaluate results against performance expectation (look back at the model built in Step 2). If expectations are not met, decide where you should spend the effort to gain some execution time.

Even when you carefully capture all the information, it's often not sufficient and you need more data to locate the problem (look at "Step 3: Performance Instrumentation" on page 125). This generates a phase in which performance tests are repeated often, varying one element at a time and keeping the environment stable. Even though you don't improve performance here, you gain understanding of what may impact performance.

The better the performance model is, the shorter this phase. By spending the time up-front, you'll save time and money at the end of the development phase. (It's important to keep the analyze-improve test cycle as short as possible, and automation is key to that.)

When the analysis has been improved, you'll be able to identify where the problem lies. For instance, platform-configuration issues may have to be fixed before application-development issues. So, analysis doesn't have to focus on application first. Plan a first stage that focuses on the platform itself. Project teams might spend two weeks fixing platform-configuration issues, such as network switches or operating-systems parameterization that delay the final delivery and impact the project budget.

Step 6: Performance Enhancements

After you have identified the performance-relevant factors and understood the underlying mechanics, you can focus on improving performance.

First, the initial result often shows that the application is 10 to 100 times slower than expected. Improving performance significantly is relatively easy at the beginning of the exercise, and becomes harder as you improve performance (Figure 35).

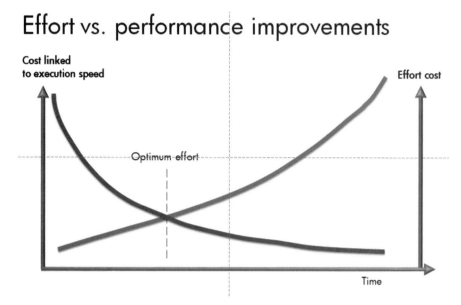

Effort vs. performance improvements

Figure 35: Optimum testing effort

Evaluate what needs to be achieved at the beginning of the testing phase. Gaining one order of magnitude is reasonable at the beginning of the testing phase. Winning two orders of magnitude is more of a challenge.

Load Testing

Load testing is not performance testing, although the two are often confused. Performance testing involves the execution speed of an application, regardless of the number of users. In load testing, we're trying to determine whether the performance data we've collected is still valid with an increasing number of users (the load). So load testing adds concurrency to the speed of the application as it is performance tested.

Load testing is specific to applications built to support several simultaneous users accessing the same instance. This testing is not for desktop applications, but for server based-applications (web applications, data-centric applications) or technical applications meant to manage a high data volume (Supervisory Control and Data Acquisition, telecommunication).

Increasing the load affects performance, so delivering unchanged performances requires the architecture to scale up. This ability has to be verified along with the basic load support. Scalability has to be specified in the same way as load. If architecture is based on vertical silos, each of them is sized to support a certain load.

Again, it's important to turn the non-functional requirements into business requirements. The definition of load scenarios and the quality gate for the load test depends largely on doing that, and every misinterpretation can increase costs significantly.

Based on the example we used at the beginning of this chapter, we can derive the load-test requirements as follows:

- The system must support 10,000 simultaneous connections with no performance impact.

- The system can support up to 11,000 simultaneous connections with a performance decrease of 1%.

Any connections above 11,000 are rejected unless it is a VIP accessing the system. In that case, a low-priority connection is closed to avoid impact on performance. Load testing is typically split into these sub-phases (Figure 36):

1. Stability

2. Load support

3. Scalability

4. Sustainability

5. Overload behavior

Figure 36: Load testing steps

Step 1: Stability

Before beginning full load testing, the system must demonstrate enough stability to sustain load.

First, perform a smoke test for every application forwarded for load testing to find out if it has any obvious flaws or errors. Then, especially for new applications, find out whether it has the capacity to support concurrent accesses.

Typically, systems have problems with shared resources and, as soon as several users access them, locking mechanisms to ensure data integrity may cause deadlocks that stop the whole application or reduce the performance significantly.

In a simple example using the flight-booking system, two agents both want to book the same flight, which has plenty of space, for different people.

- Both execute the booking at the same time.

- Agent A's process accesses the customer database first and locks it in order to input the customer data.

- Agent B's process acknowledges that the customer database is locked and, to save time, delays that access and accesses the flight database to get the flight data.

- Now both processes have to wait for the other to unlock the database and we have deadlock.

Real-world situations are much more complex: Critical sections must be identified and tests must be conducted in such a way that several instances of the application enter the critical section simultaneously and try to access shared resources at the same time. Statistically, the difficulty of meeting the case increases with the number of users, so increasing the load on the application increases the risk of deadlock.

It's important to go through this test phase to make sure all the deadlock conditions are raised and errors fixed.

Step 2: Load Support

After checking that the system is reliable and able to support load, we can start load testing. Tooling simulates users accessing the system and performing actions concurrently. When we know the system is reliable, we check the evolution of performance, which is linked to load increase.

In load testing, at least in the initial phase, the objective is not to check that a lot of test cases are run successfully, but to run a few tests and collect as much data as possible to analyze the correlation of measurement done at different levels with metrics such as CPU consumption, disk-accesses, memory consumption, and I/O.

> The correlation is built on time — the load generated is synchronized with the data collected at the same time inside the system.

During analysis, you can correlate the external event with the internal data using software like HP Load Runner, which helps drive load testing and saves a lot of analysis time. The tools also have scripting capabilities, a means to automate test replay.

Building a performance model is important. By defining the various elements (applications, databases, disks, I/O, network), the performance model allows us to identify the specific points to focus on and what to verify, which helps you build the load-testing plan.

The use-case model also helps define the typical usage of the system in order to work out a realistic and meaningful scenario. For example, if the system is to provide mostly read-access to data and very few updates, test scenarios stressing the update mechanism are low priority.

Now that testing scenarios are built, it's time to run tests. At this point, you should have them scripted so you can repeat them easily.

The usual way to conduct load tests is to increase the load gradually and check how the system reacts to the increase. This can be a visual check first — look at the response time perceived by end users, or watch indicators such as CPU or I/O in real time.

As the system shows it can handle load, we have to record test execution and capture the indicators' values as the load increases, in order to analyze them after the test is complete.

To see the mechanics behind the observed test results, it's better to increase the load gradually and allow time between each increase, so you can create identifiable steps. Initial load increase usually adds one user at a time first, then larger groups of 10 or 100 users to repeat the test.

After testing load support by increasing the load, relax the system by reducing the load and look at whether the system consumes the same resources as it did at the beginning of the test. A good verification is to increase load again to check that the system is consuming resources at the same level as it was initially. If this is not the case, you may have resources such as memory or release-management issues.

We have repeatedly pointed out the need for appropriate tools to perform load testing. It's even more important when you consider test results analysis. Without tools for graphical analysis, you'll have user perception and data tables containing thousands of measures to analyze. Acquire or build a tool that displays data graphs and correlates the various measures. With the right tools, you can investigate why performance suddenly drops. Is it CPU? Memory overload? The tools will tell you.

When you locate a problem, diagnose the issue, fix the problem, and restart.

Initially, the cause may be simple to fix (typically, it's a matter of tuning database indexes). This may seem so simple that you think it won't happen to you. But there are people who've spent their careers working at index level, tuning the database in one project and the next.

You may think that after the first test, you should investigate several directions and make modifications all at once. Not so; do it only if you have absolute confidence that it will improve load support and performance. Even in that case, you should progress step by step, as any modification may not have the expected result.

Each modification must be documented before being implemented. This may seem overkill, but after having implemented several modifications, you need to know what has been done. Document any modifications you considered and rejected. You want to avoid various people coming up with the same "good ideas," and slowing down the testing activity.

Now you can see that load testing is a progressive improvement, made of a lot of iterations of this cycle: test –> analyze –> enhance. Automation and tooling are the keys to keeping load testing in line with plans.

Step 3: Scalability

At some point, a system should be able to cope with the required load, and the system performs according to the expectation. The purpose of scalability is to support more load by adding more resources to the platform. Consider these solutions:

- Horizontal scalability — when load increase is supported through a targeted application solution

- Vertical scalability — when the solution is architected in silos, each able to handle a known load

Scalability testing requires that you verify through real-size activity that scalability is achieved as expected.

For example, if load increase can be handled by simply adding memory and CPUs, scalability testing will prove that the scalability model is right or that it's not. Scalability models usually consider that if one CPU is able to handle 100, n CPUs will handle $x \times n \times 100$ with $0<x<1$. The power of the CPUs will be spent partly on synchronization management.

You'd like x to be as close to 1 as possible to reach perfect linear scalability. But that's not what experience shows — scalability is rarely infinitely linear, x is not constant and it will decrease as n increases. The question is: Up to when? Scalability testing helps find the answer. Test the scalability model by doing what would be done in a real case: add the needed resources to support more load, and verify that the load is effectively supported (Figure 37).

Building a scalable platform is expensive, so you'll tend to limit the number of measurement points. For example, if scalability is achieved by adding CPUs, you may want to go for up to four CPUs, and see if you observe a linear scalability. That may be all you need.

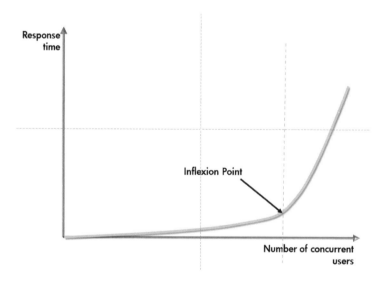

Figure 37: Scalability model

Push your tests to the point where you see the curve inflexion. It may require some hardware you don't have, so discuss this testing with your hardware provider, who can size platforms accordingly.

It's critical to find the inflexion point. One team had a project where scalability testing was performed on a 4-CPU bow that showed perfect scalability. They purchased a $600,000 license for an in-memory database, which they had to install on a 16-CPU box. You can imagine the team's reaction when they discovered that the solution was not scaling up above 8 CPUs. Working night and day did not help address the issue in the in-memory database that could not be fixed.

Involve a third party in your testing activity. You should have carried out all the previous steps so you're really testing scalability and not load-support issues.

Step 4: Sustainability

You've tested that your system can handle load and scale up, so now you have to check that it's able to sustain load over the long run. The objective is to learn whether your system, going through cycles of load increase and decrease, will consume memory.

The test scenario is again pretty simple:

- Launch your application, look at the memory size, increase load, and execute standard processes.

- Then reduce load and look the memory size used by the application.

The two values — memory size at test start and memory size at test end — should be the same.

Memory-checking tools can track memory usage. These tools will let you know if some memory that should have been released has not been when you manage memory directly in your application. If you're making use of virtual machines, look to the machine memory-management policy and check which inactive objects you should release.

At the end of sustainability testing, your system should be able to operate during months, if not years, without interruption, and you should be able to close the load-testing activity.

Step 5: Overload

The last load-testing activity is to verify system behavior when it's overloaded. Even though you've clearly shown the system in a certain configuration is able to support a certain load, you have to make sure your system won't crash during overload.

Depending on the system purpose, you may have three alternatives during overload conditions:

- Interrupt the system up to the load that can be handled again.

- Continue service delivery to all users, but degrade the service level potentially to all users, resulting in service level agreement (SLA) degradation.

- Continue service delivery to only connected users and reject any new connection over the defined limit.

Make the consequences clear to system users so they can decide which alternative is the most appropriate. For instance, a system was built during a major sporting event to let people buy last-minute tickets for matches the following day. The company selling the tickets wanted customers to buy tickets online, and the system was built and tested according to the rules. When it was time to test overload, the customer was warned and asked what should be done. The answer: "Nothing." The consequence of doing nothing was documented and the customer informed that no one might be able to buy tickets during overload. That's what happened, and it was reported in the newspapers.

Availability Testing

First, we have to understand what availability means. After we describe how availability is expressed and how availability works in the real life, we can explain how to test availability.

Expressing Availability

The usual customer request is that the system you provide must be highly available, or that system maintenance must not impact operations. So, availability is often expressed in subjective terms: The system must be available enough for the user to do what needs to be done.

One way to express availability is to use percentage representation of up-time. So we're asked to make a system available 99% of the time, 99.99% of the time or 99.999% of the time (also known as five-nine availability). Some systems must be always available, such as nuclear-power plant control-and-command systems, defense systems, and air traffic control. This is an availability that has to cope with disaster recovery.

Disaster recovery doesn't necessarily mean that the system won't interrupt in case of disaster (flooding, fire, earthquake, plane crash). It usually means that a procedure must be in place that allows the operations to restart at the point they were interrupted, within a limited time set. The time set can be 0, meaning that even in the case of a disaster, the system must not stop.

Does it mean that an earthquake must be simulated during the testing phase to demonstrate that the system is compliant with the disaster recovery requirements? Does it mean that you have to crash a plane? No.

A company building containers for nuclear material wanted containers that could be transported by plane. One condition was that the container would not break if the plane crashed. So the company tested the container falling from 4,000 meters and found it would not let the nuclear material it contained to have contact with the atmosphere. So the test was successful, but the controlling agency asked: "What would happen if the container fell within the plane?" And the agency requested the container be tested by having it crash in a plane. The company stopped the program — the test was too expensive.

This true story helps us understand that the tests required must be listed, evaluated, and agreed to at the earliest possible stage. The company would have saved significant time and money if they had, up-front, realized that one of the requirements mandated a test that it could not afford.

- Total availability, is pretty clear: the system must never stop, and no maintenance operations can interrupt the operation. Expected interventions must not alter availability, and unexpected events must not cause systems interruption.

- Availability percentage leads often to arguments. How does the percentage apply? Is it per day? Is it per month? In fact usually it is understood that the percentage should apply on a year of operation and should give a yearly unavailability.

Availability	%	99%	99,9%	9,99%	99.999%
Downtime allowed in	days	3,65	0,365	0,0365	0,00365
Downtime allowed in	hours	87,6	8,76	0,876	0,0876
Downtime allowed in	minutes	5256	525,6	52,56	5,256

Table 4: Availability time correspondence

Table 4 shows the downtime in various units (days, hours, minutes) in a year of operation, depending on the availability ratio.

- A 99% availability means the system can stop during 3.5 days in a year.

- A 99.9% availability means the system can stop only 8 hours, 45 minutes in a year.

- Five-nine (99.999%) allows no more than five minutes downtime in a year.

Usually downtime covers everything — maintenance, as well as unexpected events. So a five-nine availability means that whatever happens, incident or accident, the system does not stop and the service is still delivered. But this doesn't mean that users will see nothing. At some point, end users may be impacted, but not through service interruption.

In the next chapter, we'll see how preserving availability may or may not impact service delivery.

Turning Availability Rate into Concrete Terms

How do you prove that a system is available as is required? What tests do you run to demonstrate that the system meets availability requirements? You don't want to run your system during a full year to demonstrate that it was not down more than the allowed time.

- **Availability during maintenance.** The availability requirements may imply that maintenance activity during operations, such as upgrades or configuration modifications, must not interrupt the service.

- **Failure handling.** Any unexpected failure that could happen during operations, such as disk failure, memory failure, or CPU failure, is handled and does not interrupt the service.

We're not attempting to define how this can be achieved, but how it must be tested.

Maintenance Activities

As seen in Chapter 5, the availability requirements determine the acceptable downtime the system can suffer.

If the availability requirements state that the system must be 99% available, you have three and a half days of unavailability to perform planned maintenance activities. If it takes a day to perform a full system upgrade, you may perform three upgrades in a year, if upgrading is the only maintenance activity planned on your system.

You must then check the cumulated downtime induced by the maintenance operation as specified in the requirements. This downtime must not exceed the downtime stipulated by the availability requirements.

Failures can occur during the maintenance activity, so plan for recovery procedures that would let the operations be retried later on.

When availability requirements stipulate that the system availability must be 99.999%, there is no downtime possible for maintenance activities. In this case, all maintenance activities must be run as the system is running. No interruption is possible.

Failure Handling

Handling failures in a highly available context means simulating system failures to demonstrate that your system continues to operate, making sure there is no single point of failure that will cause the whole service to stop.

Obviously, failure has an impact. How much of an impact, and where, is dependent on the architecture you put in place. Your customer may require that the service must not be impacted by a single failure. That usually means that if one part of the system is failing, the remaining resources will handle all the load the system has to support.

You can deliver this capability by building a platform with more resources than are needed for normal operation, so if one element of a resource pool fails, the remaining set will provide enough power for the system to deliver service as usual. If N is the number of resource instances needed to deliver the service, $N+1$ will be used to deliver the service. This is known as "single-failure support." If two instances fail at the same time, the service will be impacted, but it's statistically improbable that two instances will fail at the same time.

What about a five-nine compliancy requirement? The failure detection and the fail-over execution take some time, during which the customer may feel some impact. Consider then that five-nine means you should be able to detect failures and perform fail-over quickly. A system can be considered five-nine compliant if load support is degraded but the service remains available.

The level of availability depends on the time needed to detect failures and perform fail-over. But when a failure has occurred, a broken resource needs to be replaced and that replacement may also impact availability. So high availability does not only relate to failure, but also to what's needed to bring the system back to its initial operational condition. All the downtime incurred during each of these steps will factor into the availability level (Figure 38).

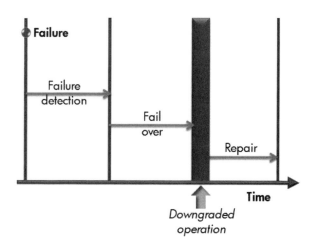

Figure 38: Failure impact on operations

Now that we've seen how availability works in real-world conditions, how do we test it?

High Availability Testing

If a system is still operating when one resource item fails, this system provides a level of availability. The availability level can be deduced from the time spent in each of the three phases, as shown in the figure above, and the operations required for system maintenance don't break the availability requirements.

Maintenance Operation Testing

Availability requirements may imply that operations actions, such as system upgrades or backups, can be performed without interrupting the service delivered by the tested system.

This testing phase aims to execute all maintenance activities and check that they are performed either in the agreed time-frame, or can be performed without stopping the service. Always consider that problems may occur during maintenance activities, requiring the system to be able to retreat to a safe status where it can run.

Failure Management Testing

In high availability scenarios, it's important that failures are correctly detected. Two situations have to be evaluated:

- A failure is detected effectively when it occurs (that is, the failure does not remain undetected).

- Failures are not detected inconsistently (that is, the system is not detecting failures when there is no failure).

We test the first case by simulating predictable failures (described below) and making sure they are detected and mitigated quickly enough to meet the requirements. We have to evaluate all potential failure conditions and produce these failures while testing the system, even though it can be tedious to identify failure conditions, which involve a detailed study of the business-process execution.

> The moment at which a specific failure occurs plays an important role.

For each failure condition, you may have several test cases that will all relate to different points of failure occurrence. It's often difficult to produce or simulate the failure at the exact time specified, which usually corresponds to a specific step in the system. This requires tooling and ad hoc development.

You'll find some tests impossible to perform (remember the nuclear waste example). But this situation too must be documented, letting management know which tests cannot be performed and they can decide what is affordable.

Inaccurate failure detection is harder to simulate because it refers to something that doesn't happen: Why would a failure be detected when it didn't occur? It can happen, for example, if a traffic spike over a communication line interrupts the connection between two parts of the system, which slows the dialogue between the two parts. If the latency is high, one or both parts may consider the communication broken and consider that a failure occurred.

Depending on the nature of the system, this scenario may be acceptable (when one part stops processing and the other part retries by repeating the request) or not (when one part performs the part of the process it was due to execute and the other part, by repeating the request, will generate duplicates).

Testing this requires that we first define the process where a failure in both parts is detected, then the "near failure" must be generated and system behavior checked.

Reliability Testing

Reliability testing is meant to verify that a system is reacting to aggressive conditions in a way that protects business operations. Let's ask some questions to illuminate what this is about.

What do aggressive conditions mean?

Aggressive conditions are unrecoverable errors occurring on the system environment. For example, full disk failure, full CPU failure, or full memory failure are events that cause the application to stop operating.

Less obvious cases can have similar effects — disk errors causing corrupted data to be stored in a database, disk errors creating a database coherency error, and so on. These don't interrupt the system, but the system has to handle unexpected data or information. This happens at a hardware level, so the application cannot filter it: It just happens.

Because it copes with very difficult conditions, reliability testing is also called "destructive testing." The objective is to test the system in conditions close to destruction.

Why is it important to test reliability?

If systems that support core business activities, such as billing, have a small disk error, it can alter the data being entered and corrupt the database. You'd expect the application to detect data corruption, report the error, and stop the system until the problem is fixed.

But in many such situations, the system fails with no error message. When we try to re-launch, the system crashes again and again before we understand what's happening and where, so we can fix the problem. Also, consider what data was lost: How many millions of entries were lost? Does anyone know?

This is why we need to conduct reliability testing: to make sure that if any unrecoverable error occurs, the system is able to detect it and eventually interrupt it to supply information on the cause.

Reliability testing is usually the activity conducted at the end of development projects, and is so often skipped. But skipping it means a lot of systems simply crash when something odd occurs.

Reliability Requirements

Think about the possible unrecoverable crash conditions and define the expected system behavior. The best approach is to ask how reliability requirements can be turned into business requirements.

Usually we can ask a simple question: how much can we afford to spend on this phase?

Consider a desktop application where the only one who sees a problem during a system failure is one end user using the software. The time spent testing reliability, as defined above, will differ from more critical systems, like a nuclear-power plant's control-and-command program. Even if a memory chip has problem, we don't want this system to become unstable. In that case, reliability testing is critical.

Usually the conditions leading to an unrecoverable error are hard to predict. We can often keep a single disk failure from impacting a system. But most of the time the error is coming from external systems, and then we have to be able to restart the system quickly from a known state, which has to be consistent.

To understand what "consistent" means here, let's consider that the error occurs in the middle of a transaction that involves payments. It cannot proceed and a roll-back is impossible. What shall we do with it then? Depending on the payment amount, several strategies may be defined:

- If the payment amount is below a defined amount, do nothing — forget the transaction. The system owner may lose some money, but it will be less expensive than trying to find a solution.

- If the transaction is greater than this amount, procedures have to be put in place at each step of the transaction, so its status is recorded and it can be retrieved when the system starts. It's worth spending more time taking care of it.

Why aren't we using one strategy to secure all transactions so if the system crashes often, we save more money? The system is not meant to fail often, so failures must remain the exception and occur certainly less than once a year. So losing a small amount should not happen often.

In some circumstances the system, despite all the care taken, is not able to restart right after the crash as the state is not consistent. What do we do then?

The first possibility is to start from a previous consistent state that can eventually be a backup. Define in the requirements the frequency at which these backups should be performed, and how to restart.

> Even though a daily or hourly backup is performed, if a system is handling millions of transactions an hour, the financial consequences may be dramatic if the past transactions are not recovered.

It should be possible, when the latest backup has been restored, to re-apply each transaction. This requires time and the tools to help perform the task effectively.

This is just an example of how to handle reliability. Requirements may be that users are not impacted, so when the back-end of a front-end/back-end architecture fails, the front-end is still able to provide degraded service, which in turn needs to be specified.

We don't want to consider failures, and often this activity is not conducted thoroughly. But those of you who've had to handle a system crash on Christmas Eve know very well why failures must always be considered.

Reliability Testing

Conducting reliability testing is a difficult and painful process:

- Difficult because errors must be generated at some precise execution points.

- Painful because after you've generated the error, the initial results are not what you expect — many errors must be generated to understand what happened and design the correction.

To be efficient, you must design code so the error interrupts execution at various steps. Distributed architectures make this more difficult, requiring synchronization between distributed components. This is different from real conditions, but there are few other options.

On top of this, although you can implement synchronization in your system, it's more difficult to synchronize external components (those you are not implementing). So repeat the same test case often through various points of interruption -- test automation is a must.

Non-Functional Testing Critical for Success

Now we know why non-functional testing is essential for businesses that cannot afford a system failure. Our step-by-step process can help you evaluate what you need to test for, and when, in your development cycle. Knowing ahead how you'll cope with a load spike or how reliable your business-critical systems are when events like power failure or earthquake occur is a sound investment in time and resources.

Even though non-functional testing has to occur late in your development lifecycle, after you know that all components of your system work functionally, taking care of the non-functional aspects can make or break your project or business.

Chapter 7

Application Security Testing: The Next Frontier

As unfathomable amounts of information are created, accessed, tracked, and shared among users and enterprises, security is a primary concern that's rapidly becoming more important and more complex. Application security is one of the most challenging situations an enterprise must cope with, and it will become more and more critical as the world grows more interconnected.

Security testing has become so much more important now than when we wrote the first edition of *Optimize Quality for Business Outcomes, A Practical Approach to Software Testing,* we are devoting a whole chapter to it. Multidimensional security challenges exist today that were not on the radar even three years ago — the technology, the attacks, and even the attackers' motives are constantly evolving. And there is no single silver-bullet approach that addresses the entire range of security threats.

The sheer scope and complexity of security issues can baffle and paralyze IT leaders, and they often delegate the responsibility for secure data and systems to specialists.

For many issues, such as determining enterprise security policies or selecting the right firewall, turning to experts can be a reasonable approach — security teams have the skills to identify the problems and the ability to implement solutions. But ensuring web application security goes beyond specialists' ability to handle, even if they understand the problem.

Web applications are where security and privacy meet. In an increasingly interconnected world, this intersection comprises the biggest and most complex set of security challenges (attacks, risks, and regulations) for today's enterprise.

> Web application security is a major business challenge and a complex technical problem all rolled into one.

This chapter explores the imperative of application security — its origins, what it means to the business and technology teams, and how companies can handle the challenge today and going forward. (Chapter 7 is merely an introduction — several excellent books in our Reference section cover the topic in greater detail.)

Understanding the Application Security Problem

As with any significant problem, you can't devise the right solution without first understanding the nature, causes, and impact of the problem.

Application security has three major dimensions.

- Technical: Why are web applications vulnerable?
- Process (or lifecycle): Where do these vulnerabilities come from, and how can they be eliminated?
- Business: Do these security threats really matter to the business?

The Technical Problem

Hackers targeting a web application can launch very sophisticated attacks, and it's tempting to assume that only security gurus can understand the technical elements of security. But it all really boils down to two simple things:

- The web application breaches the enterprise perimeter— it is, and must be, a trusted conduit to sensitive data and capabilities behind the firewalls.

- The client end of the web application is controlled by the user, not by the enterprise.

Why is this combination a lethal one?

> In this one-two punch hackers have complete control over one end of this trusted chain. By manipulating data, logic, and communications at the client end, they can mine and manipulate data and resources inside the perimeter.

Let's look more closely at both aspects of the situation to see what can be done to mitigate or eliminate the issues without touching the applications themselves.

Figure 39 illustrates a typical web application and enterprise security configuration. It shows how the application connects and communicates with the database through the web and app servers. Although three firewalls exist, and traffic is restricted to specific ports and protocols, the application itself still connects to the inside of the corporate database. Other traffic is blocked, but the application's traffic goes through in a trusted chain.

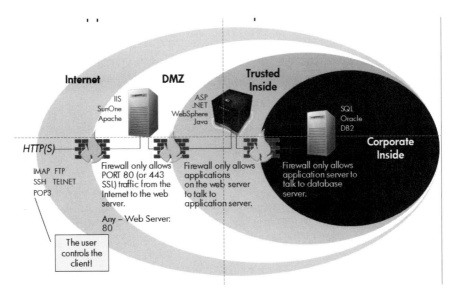

Figure 39: Web applications breach the perimeter

Can we simply shut down the web application or at least its access to resources and information inside the perimeter? More functionality and access mean more potential vulnerabilities, and if functions will be little used, they may not be worth keeping.

> One important aspect of the application-security strategy is to limit the functionality and access of applications to only what's truly necessary.

Most times, however, shutting down or severely limiting the application's access to resources and information inside the perimeter is not an option, because enabling users to do things like check bank balances, order products, book air travel, pay bills, or create accounts is the point of the application.

So, can something be done on the client end to address the problem?

Unfortunately, the fundamental architecture of the web, with its open standards, gives hackers what they need to see and manipulate the data, logic, and communication that touch the client. They use editors, debuggers, sniffers, scanners, and a wide variety of utilities to facilitate attacks.

> In effect, hackers leverage the application's ability to get past the barriers that would otherwise be in their way.

Hackers only need to look for and exploit any "open doors and windows" to get in and steal what's inside the perimeter. And, the major trends in web applications only make the challenge more difficult.

First, more functionality and data from inside the perimeter are being exposed by web applications. Websites have evolved from online brochures to increasingly sophisticated, business-critical systems in which users can now do nearly everything on the web that was once only available through internal systems.

Second, a massive refresh of web applications into rich internet applications, based on techniques like AJAX and technologies like Flex, multiplies the security issues. More logic and data exist at the client in a rich internet application, giving the bad guys more ammunition with which to attack the application. Perhaps more importantly, many of the code snippets and widgets developers use to build these new applications come from code they got from others, or from the internet.

> ■ The good news is developers can build sexy, interactive web applications much faster.
> ■ The bad news is this leveraged code is likely to be rife with security vulnerabilities.

The net result is that applications, particularly web applications, have become the soft underbelly of security for an enterprise leading to all kinds of application-oriented attacks. Table 5 gives short descriptions of the top 10 types of attacks and the resulting threats, as tracked by the Open Web Application Security Project (OWASP).

1 - cross site scripting (XSS)	XSS flaws occur whenever an application takes user-supplied data and sends it to a web browser without first validating or encoding that content. XSS allows attackers to execute script in the victim's browser that can hijack user sessions, deface websites, or introduce worms.
2 - injection flaws	Injection flaws, particularly SQL injection, are common in web applications. Injection occurs when a command or query sends user-supplied data to an interpreter. The attacker's hostile data tricks the interpreter into executing unintended commands or changing data.
3 - malicious file execution	Code vulnerable to remote file inclusion (RFI) allows attackers to include hostile code and data, resulting in devastating attacks, such as total server compromise. Malicious file execution attacks affect PHP, XML, and any framework that accepts filenames or files from users.
4 - insecure direct object reference	A direct object reference occurs when a developer exposes a reference to an internal implementation object (a file, directory, database record, or key) as a URL or form parameter. Attackers can manipulate those references to access other objects without authorization.

Table 5: Top 10 web application vulnerabilities for 2007

5 - cross site request forgery (CSRF)	A CSRF attack forces a logged-on victim's browser to send a pre-authenticated request to a vulnerable web application, which then forces the victim's browser to perform a hostile action to the benefit of the attacker. CSRF can be as powerful as the web application it attacks.
6 - information leakage and improper error handling	Applications can unintentionally leak information about their configuration and internal workings, or violate privacy through a variety of application problems. Attackers use this weakness to steal sensitive data or conduct more serious attacks.
7 - broken authentication and session management	Account credentials and session tokens are often not properly protected. Attackers compromise passwords, keys, or authentication tokens to assume other users' identities.
8 - insecure cryptographic storage	Web applications rarely use cryptographic functions properly to protect data and credentials. Attackers use weakly protected data to conduct identity theft and other crimes, such as credit card fraud.
9 - insecure communications	Applications frequently fail to encrypt network traffic when it's necessary to protect sensitive communications.
10 - failure to restrict URL access	Applications often only protect sensitive functionality by preventing the display of links or URLs to unauthorized users. Attackers can use this weakness to access and perform unauthorized operations by accessing those URLs directly.

Table 5: Top 10 web application vulnerabilities for 2007 (continued)

These vulnerabilities help explain why, according to Gartner, 75 percent of attacks now occur at the application layer. With as many as 85 percent of websites vulnerable to attack, it is no wonder that the attackers have shifted their focus to web applications as an entry point into corporate networks and databases.

Combine all this with the explosion in the number and scope of web applications, and it's not surprising that we've seen a dramatic rise in the number of overall attacks. (See Figure 40.)

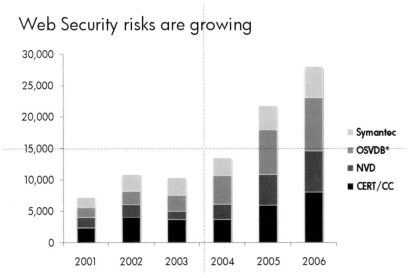

Figure 40: Rise in application attacks

The nature of the attacks shown in Table 5 also reveal the final critical fault — security vulnerabilities exist in the applications themselves. When we combine this critical fact with the need for applications to breach the perimeter and the uncontrolled client, we understand the answer to our question: Where do these vulnerabilities come from in the first place?

Anatomy of a Web Application Attack

To prevent an application attack, you must first understand how a hacker thinks.

Act 1: The scan

A hacker begins by running a port scan to detect the open HTTP and HTTPS ports for each server and then retrieves the default page from each open port.

Act 2: Information gathering

The hacker identifies the type of server running on each port and parses each page to find normal links (HTML anchors). This lets the hacker determine the structure of the site and the logic of the application.

The hacker then analyzes the found pages and checks for comments and other useful data that may reference files and directories not intended for public use.

Act 3: Testing

The hacker goes through a testing process for each of the application scripts or dynamic functions of the application, looking for development errors in order to gain further access into the application.

Act 4: Planning the attack

After identifying all the information available through passive (undetectable) means, the hacker selects and deploys attacks.

These attacks focus on the information gained from the passive, information-gathering process.

Act 5: Launching the attack

The hacker attacks each web application identified as vulnerable during the initial review of your site.

Results

The results of the attack can include lost data, content manipulation, theft, and loss of customers. The average corporation cannot detect such attacks and may use significant resources trying to diagnose the implications of an attack.

The Lifecycle Problem

The previous section begins to shed some light on why application security poses an extraordinary new security challenge. The vulnerabilities are in the applications themselves — the security issues are "baked into" the applications, which means the security solution can't be "bolted on."

In a very real way, security issues are like any other type of application defect. They are injected into applications early in the lifecycle during the design and development phase, but only create significant business risk when the applications go live and are used in production. Unlike other defects, however, security threats evolve. So, we need to look more closely at the characteristics of the lifecycle to ensure that our solution addresses both the root cause of security vulnerabilities and the constantly evolving threats.

When you examine lifecycle issues, four key considerations emerge.

- The security challenge touches many stakeholders to different degrees during the lifecycle.

- Development and QA teams must play a central role in securing applications.

- When multiple stakeholders have to synchronize, good process and policies drive success.

- We must understand the lifecycle phases, as the nature of each phase impacts the solution.

Multiple stakeholders: Any lifecycle problem invariably involves multiple stakeholders across the organization. Beyond security teams, developers, quality assurance groups, architects, and business analysts play important roles in creating and delivering applications.

Development and QA teams: The skill sets of developers and QA teams must become part of the security solution — they work at the critical phase where security issues enter the application. Now that we see where the problems come from, it should be easy to tell developers and quality assurance teams to stop them at the source. Unfortunately, it's not.

> **Developers and QA teams are not trained security experts, and they never will be.**

All the training, education, and experience for these pivotal roles lead to specific capabilities.

- Developers know how to create application capabilities.
- Quality assurance teams validate capabilities and user/ data error handling — they are taught to think like the business or end user (but not like hackers).
- Performance assurance groups know how to identify application performance issues and bottlenecks, and optimize performance and scalability.

Hackers think differently than developers and quality/performance teams. They do things users would never do and that developers and QA teams cannot conceive of. And while security teams (your existing experts) may have some understanding of the hacker mindset and techniques, they are not developers, usually don't have access to the code, and couldn't possibly keep up with the volume of applications even if they did.

> **Training is only part of the answer.**

Microsoft may be able to put all its developers and quality teams through extensive security retraining, but few, if any enterprise IT organizations can pull that off. That's a reality, but the solution must still bring security expertise into the equation. Here's how.

Process and policies: Whenever multiple stakeholders all need to do the right things at the right times, the processes and policies you put in place provide the foundation for success or failure.

Lifecycle phases: It's important to understand the lifecycle phases for two reasons. One, the major phases have markedly different characteristics, which the solution must account for.

> The processes, time, costs, and risks are very different in the development and testing phase from the production phase of an application.

And two, application security creates perhaps the most unique lifecycle problem technology teams have ever faced. New attacks are created constantly, so constant vigilance and continuous vulnerability assessment updates are necessary.

> Systems that were perfectly secure yesterday are vulnerable today, even though your teams have changed nothing.

Now that we understand the technical and lifecycle aspects of the security problem, let's look at the impact of application security on the business.

The Business Problem

The technical problem and the lifecycle problem wouldn't matter if there were little or no impact to the business. Unfortunately, application security is a huge business problem in terms of:

- Brand damage
- Legal and compliance issues
- Direct and indirect costs of security breaches and remediation

Each of these areas is compelling by itself and can exact a significant toll on the business. Combine all three, and it's easy to see why application security is now at the top of the priority list for the CFO, CEO, CIO, and CISO.

Brand damage from a security breach or data loss can be difficult to quantify, and it will vary by company and industry.

> Customers' fears of identity theft and privacy loss are mounting and the costs to switch to a competitor are fairly trivial, so most companies work very hard to keep their names out of damaging headlines.

A quick web search yields many examples of companies who have suffered security breaches and logged major costs in time, energy, dollars, and customers.

Addressing application security goes beyond just good business sense: in an increasing number of industries and countries, it is the law. Regulatory risk is substantial and growing concern. Failure to adhere to a growing list of government and industry rules can lead to fines, discontinuation of services, and even civil and criminal penalties. The following common regulations all emphasize the need for security, especially at the application level.

- **Payment Card Industry Data Security Standards (PCI DSS):** Backed by major credit card companies, PCI DSS outlines various security controls, which must be adhered to by any entity processing, storing, or transmitting credit card numbers. Failure to comply with PCI DSS can lead to payment card processing privileges being revoked.

- **California Bill 1386 (CA1386):** Requires any business with operations or customers in California to meet strict standards for the protection of private customer information. A potential breach in security requires public notification of each affected individual or customer, thereby ensuring that negative publicity is all but unavoidable. Civil and/or criminal penalties have yet to be determined.

■ **Sarbanes-Oxley:** Mandates that senior management must accept personal responsibility for reviewing all financial statements for accuracy and legal compliance. Because poor security practices make these assurances impossible to prove, public corporations are now forced to document security practices at all levels of the organization.

Add to these, HIPAA (healthcare), Gramm-Leach-Bliley (banking), European Union privacy regulations, and an ever-increasing number of other legislative initiatives, and the need for demonstrable, verifiable application security becomes acute.

These regulations create an environment in which organizations must prove that all reasonable measures for security are verifiable and functional. Senior management may face corporate or personal responsibility when a security incident occurs, but proof of best practices can only be established when line managers, individual programmers, and QA professionals can demonstrate their own best practices.

For the first time, the application-development process itself has become part of corporate governance and regulatory compliance.

> Web application security is now a business quality issue.

Secure coding practices significantly reduce threats to confidentiality, integrity, and availability. Insecure code opens organizations to potential legal, regulatory, and shareholder liability. Those individuals responsible for selecting, developing, testing, and deploying web applications must now be prepared to help their employers answer for any lapses in security resulting from poorly written and/or inadequately tested web applications.

Security breaches have significant quantifiable costs:

- The 2007 CSI Computer Crime and Security Survey found that the average reported loss among survey respondents amounted to $350,424 — more than a two-fold increase from the previous year.

- The Ponemon Institute's 2007 Annual Study, U.S. Cost of a Data Breach, found that the average cost per lost customer record amounted to $197, for an overall average cost of $6.3 million per breach.

While these statistics are not exclusive to web application attacks, corporate web applications are a common attack vector for accessing confidential data. Industry analysts also estimate that the failure to identify and repair security vulnerabilities during the software development process can carry extra costs.

Removing a defect after software is operational can cost between 10 and 15 times as much as correcting the error within the development and QA process.

When Development and QA teams incorporate security testing, you can significantly reduce the costs of vulnerability remediation. We estimate that if 50 percent of software vulnerabilities were removed prior to production use, enterprise security management costs would be reduced by 75 percent.

Considering the risks of brand damage, the regulatory and compliance imperative, and the costs of security breaches, the need for integrating methodical security assessment into the application-delivery process becomes clear.

The Solution

Now that we understand the nature of the problem, let's look at the core principles we can use to craft the solution.

- **Principle 1: Take a systemic approach to solving this problem.** The solution must encompass:
  - security strategy and policies
  - process and practices
  - education and training
  - technology
  - all the key stakeholders in the application lifecycle

  Some elements of the solution may be more effective than others in certain circumstances, but no single security assessment mechanism is perfect. We have to figure out how to get the key elements in place and working well together.

- **Principle 2: Application security threats are constantly evolving.** Any solution for testing and assessing applications must have a mechanism in place to keep teams up to date on the latest threats, risks, and fixes.

- **Principle 3: The solution must fit into the landscape and operational flow of your application lifecycle.** If solving the security problem up-ends everything else and application work stalls, you're no better off than you were before you address the security issues — you've simply exchanged one problem for another.

Let's look at each of the major solution elements in turn, then at how to bring them all together in the right way for your enterprise.

Enterprise Security Strategy and Policies

These encompass the overall security framework of an organization and provide the foundation for an enterprise's approach to security. They form the cornerstone of an effective organization and should serve as a roadmap that every person in the organization can use in a variety of ways.

- The strategy addresses how the enterprise will approach and effect security.

- The policies answer the question of "what should be done and by whom?"

A comprehensive strategy and set of policies will touch on all aspects of security. An important subset related to data security, privacy, and compliance will drive critical security requirements and assessment processes that cut across all application projects and initiatives.

The CIO and Chief Information Security Officer (CISO) are generally the appropriate owners and should drive the development of the enterprise security strategy and policies. Several excellent references can help guide enterprises in this endeavor, including those from MSF, Computerworld, and CMU/SEI.

Because this framework is such a critical factor in the success of security efforts and security risk management/mitigation, the following three things are critical:

- Use cross-functional teams to develop the strategy and policies to get various perspectives and, most importantly, the buy-in to drive adoption through the organization.

- Establish well-thought-out metrics and key performance indicators (KPIs) to drive the right behaviors.

- Where possible, get beyond "paper docs" and embed the desired workflow into key support systems, like HP's Quality Center, to enforce and accelerate critical security-related processes.

The cross-functional team should include members from Security, Legal/Compliance, Finance, Technology Strategy and Architecture, Development, Quality Assurance, and

Operations, as well as representation from the lines of business. Seek external expertise where security knowledge and competence is at a low maturity level.

Process and Practices

Taking an application from concept to delivery involves several phases, dozens of steps, and hundreds of activities and tasks. This is not meant to be a lengthy discourse on granular process elements, nor a dictate of a single, perfect process. Rather, it's an overview and description of the core processes, with pointers to the most important considerations and elements to fold into your existing processes (if they're good), or upon which to re-engineer the processes (if they're poor).

Figure 41 below shows an overall process that incorporates the best practices described in this section. There are many parallels between security testing and more traditional quality testing, but there are also a few key differences.

Requirements

A significant similarity between security testing and assessment and more traditional software testing is that it starts with requirements. Application security requirements are determined primarily by two things:

- The relevant enterprise security policies, which are driven by security-related business risks and security/privacy compliance requirements (see Figure 41)

- The threat model and attack surface for the particular application under test

Microsoft defines threat modeling as an engineering technique used to identify threats, attacks, vulnerabilities, and countermeasures in the context of your application scenario. Wikipedia's definition is more straightforward: A threat model is the set of possible attacks to consider. There are several good references for developing threat models, including Microsoft's, which is an integral part of its Security Development Lifecycle.

The attack surface of an application is the union of code, interfaces, services, protocols, and practices available to all users, with a strong focus on what is accessible to unauthenticated users.

Analyzing and comparing the threat model with the attack surface of the application determines the security requirements specific to that application. Combining these with the enterprise policy and the core functionality requirements of the application allows you accomplish two important things.

- First, you are now able to highlight the significant threats and relate them to functionality. This enables trade-offs that can reduce the attack surface, while maintaining key application capabilities. A smaller attack surface invariably yields less risk.

- Second, this enables a risk-based approach to security testing.

Risk-based Approach

With the threat model and attack surface in hand, you can now identify and establish the risk and priority of the various security requirements. As with functional and performance requirements, this risk-based approach focuses the work of both Development and Quality teams. In any significant application project, Development and QA never have the time and/or the resources to run every possible test or assessment, so it is imperative to focus on the most critical areas.

A risk-based approach to security testing ensures that key stakeholders remain laser-focused on the highest value and highest risk business processes and security threats.

Design and Code Reviews

Many security experts advocate manual design and code reviews for security vulnerabilities. We don't recommend eliminating manual reviews, but they should be highly targeted and supplemented by effective, advanced technology.

Manual reviews present two major issues for most companies.

- The quality and utility of the reviews are based on the security expertise of the reviewers, which is often in short supply.

- The volume and velocity of both web applications and vulnerabilities make manual reviews impossible to keep up with.

Fortunately, here's where the latest technology, like HP's DevInspect software, delivers massive benefit through automation and continuous updates against the latest threats. With DevInspect to scan and assess the entire code base, manual reviews can focus on those areas of the application where they'll have the greatest impact. For example, code that handles login and access, code that handles sensitive data, and so on.

The next three process elements — developer testing, QA testing, and production scanning — are intimately related to the technology and specific testing techniques employed. Let's look at the goals of each activity, as well as similarities and differences with traditional testing. (More information on the testing techniques can also be found in Appendix A.)

Developer/Unit Security Testing

Traditionally, developers had little or no responsibility for application security, beyond things like simple access control or encryption. But because vulnerabilities lie within the applications themselves, developers are a root cause of application security problems. Therefore, one of the biggest and most important process changes is that developers must now engage in rigorous security testing of their code.

At one level, this is no different than any other type of defect; finding it and fixing it as early as possible is the best and the most cost-effective by orders of magnitude. Developers have always had responsibility for Unit testing their code for functionality and, more recently, performance issues.

One major difference — and the biggest challenge with unit-level security testing — is that developers are not, and will never really be, security experts. Fortunately, today's advanced security testing products, like HP's DevInspect, bridge this knowledge gap for the developer. These products enable the developer to accomplish the equivalent of unit security testing: finding and fixing security defects in their code before it is checked in to become part of the larger application.

Developer security testing differs from traditional unit testing in two additional important ways as a result of the security testing technology.

- Developers do not write their own security tests. Rather, they use products like DevInspect to scan and analyze their code and identify the security vulnerabilities.

- For many of the most common and highest risk security defects, developers can leverage hardened and proven code from commercial libraries, such as HP's SecureObjects, to fix the defect automatically.

Quality Assurance/System Security Testing

The story for Quality Assurance teams parallels that of the developer. To date, these groups have had very little responsibility for security testing, and they're not security experts. Yet the principle of finding and fixing defects as early as possible remains.

Quality Assurance teams exercise application functionality in integration and system tests. This is important because many defects only appear at the system level or as the application comes together from smaller parts. Security defects are no different. Thus it's critical that QA teams add comprehensive security testing to their set of responsibilities.

Advanced security products geared for QA teams enable them to do security testing during the Integration and System Test phases. Again, the QA teams do not write their own security tests, but they configure the security testing product, like HP's QAInspect, to run appropriate security scans against the application. These scans identify all known vulnerabilities.

Because QA teams are not responsible for fixing the security defect, there is no need for a SecureObjects for QA. In this sense, security defects follow the same workflow as any other defect, with one exceptional advantage: for each vulnerability, QAInspect can automatically populate defect management systems, like the one in HP's Quality Center, with detailed information about the vulnerability and how to fix it. This gives the developer a tremendous leg up in making the right fix and accelerates the entire process dramatically.

Production Security Scanning and Assessment

To the extent that application security is being addressed today, it is likely in some form of application security scanning in production environments. But even when companies add Development and QA teams as part of a comprehensive approach to application security, they must keep up their production scanning because that's where the real security business risk exists.

- Production environments are different than testing labs — some vulnerabilities will only show up here.

- Production application, system, and network changes may open up new security holes.

- New attacks are invented all the time.

Production security scanning consists of active, periodic assessments of the live web applications. One major difference between production scanning and Dev or QA security testing is that production scanning is typically driven by security experts. These experts are part of security teams that report to Operations. Hence, the products used and the types of scans are generally the most sophisticated in the enterprise.

Post-mortems, Cross-project, and Lifecycle Analyses

Perhaps the single best way to gain insight into the effectiveness of the overall application lifecycle is by post-mortem analysis on application projects. For many years, application and quality-process owners have used such analyses to identify what's working, what's broken, and how to fix it. This is particularly important for new initiatives, such as the implementation of a lifecycle approach to ensuring application security (Figure 41), but enterprises should make these analyses a standard part of the process for every application project. Doing this will enable continuous process improvement and help you identify best practices across the organization.

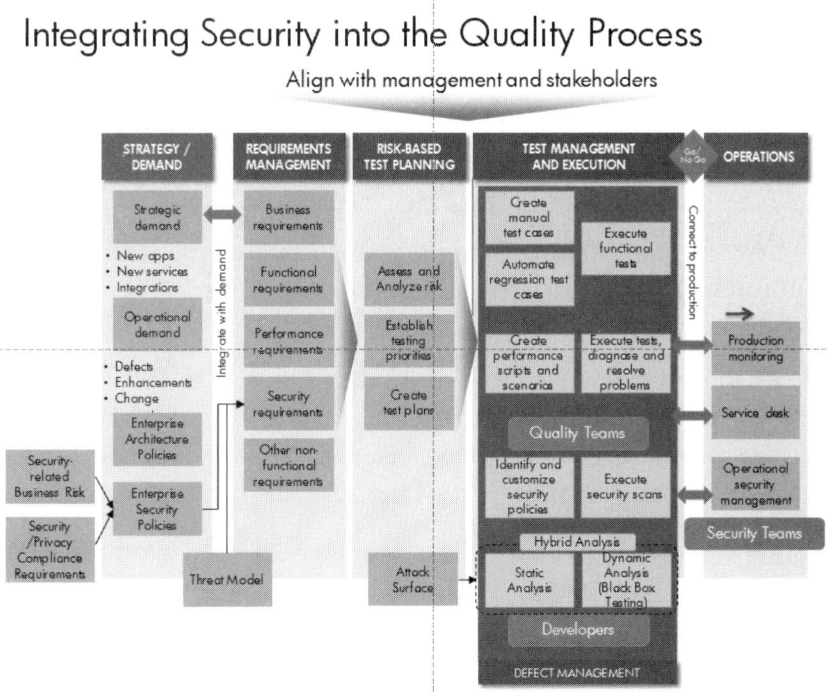

Integrating Security into the Quality Process

Align with management and stakeholders

STRATEGY / DEMAND	REQUIREMENTS MANAGEMENT	RISK-BASED TEST PLANNING	TEST MANAGEMENT AND EXECUTION		Go/ No Go	OPERATIONS

Figure 41: Security assessment and validation as part of the application delivery process

Education and Training

For most companies, it will never be practical or possible to train developers and Quality teams to be security experts. That doesn't mean education and training is unimportant, just that it's critical to understand the right role for education and training, and to focus your efforts in the right areas. The four most important are:

- The scope and scale of the security threat as related to business risk
- The purpose and use of enterprise security policies and practices
- The implementation of security assurance as a standard part of the process going forward
- The use of key security products and technology

A simple analogy might be an informed web user and anti-virus tools. Users can't become experts at virus detection and prevention on their own, but when they understand the risks and how to use the appropriate products, they can achieve the right result, which is the removal of existing virus and malware threats and effective ongoing protection.

One of the best by-products of the latest security testing solutions is that they'll help your developers and Quality teams become more educated and expert over time. Many developers admit the compiler has always been one of the best educational tools. The same concept holds true for today's security testing technology.

Key Stakeholders

Most of the key stakeholders can be traced fairly easily from the steps and elements in the overall process.

- Development
- Quality Assurance
- Security teams

- Security liaison
- CISO
- Application owners
- Business representatives
- Compliance officer and teams

Many leading companies create a security liaison role to bridge the gap between the security teams, which work in Operations, and the Development and Quality teams, which sit upstream. It's especially important in the beginning, when security testing makes its way upstream into the application delivery process.

Finally, successful companies create a culture that recognizes security is everyone's responsibility. As a result, all the stakeholders know the strategy, policies, processes, and their role and responsibility with respect to security.

Technology

The right technology is a fundamental enabler of the vitally important security testing and validation activities. Without the advanced security assessment products now available, development and QA teams could not be brought into the process of securing applications. And securing applications would be an extraordinarily expensive, hit-or-miss proposition.

HP's Application Security Center solution addresses key security assessment technologies and the techniques they support. (Find more details about the HP solution in Appendix B.)

Five key technology elements support application security initiatives:

- Static analysis
- Dynamic analysis
- Hybrid analysis
- Secure code libraries
- Continuously updated security knowledge-bases

Static Analysis (aka Source Code Analysis)

Source code analysis products use a technique called variable tracing. Developers use these tools to inject test data into the application during security testing to study the software's potential values and behaviors through the call graphs that represent data flows through the application. By injecting test data this way, the source code analysis product infers what behavior may occur for a certain scenario and variable value. Some refer to this technology as an inference engine.

The danger of the source code analysis technique is that it produces inferences, or guesses, as to how the system might behave during run-time and production configuration conditions.

> Developers who rely on source code analysis to infer security problems in the application must perform additional security testing to validate the application's real run-time behavior with respect to potential vulnerabilities.

Dynamic Analysis (aka Black-Box Testing)

Also known as automated penetration or fuzz testing, *dynamic analysis* occurs when a security tool actively attacks the running application based on thousands of known vulnerabilities and attack patterns. A dynamic analysis tool executes thousands of hack attempts on the application in a matter of minutes, simulating what a hacker would do over days or weeks.

The dynamic analysis approach can be less thorough than source code analysis because it does not have access to, or detailed knowledge of, the application source code.

Hybrid Analysis

Analysis tools, such as source code analysis or dynamic analysis, are alone only a partial solution. To increase the reliability of security testing results, security testing should be a combination of analysis techniques — utilizing source code analysis information to direct a second, more practical approach called dynamic analysis. This allows developers to identify vulnerabilities more accurately and confidently than with either technique individually. This combination approach, known as *hybrid analysis*, produces the accurate and reliable security information that developers need to assess the security of their code.

Secure Code Libraries

Almost all software attacks depend on input that's processed in an unexpected manner. Thus, the holy grail of software security is airtight input validation. Strangely, many developers continue to build their own input validation routines, and companies may end up with literally hundreds of variants. Few, if any, developers write their own encryption libraries instead of using market-proven ones, but too many fail to leverage similar libraries for the other critical aspects of application security. This is almost certainly explained by ignorance of both the threats and the solution.

One of the best examples of secure code libraries is SecureObjects, from HP's security researchers and expert developers. SecureObjects is a proven, secure set of code libraries to help developers harden and secure their applications.

Continuously Updated Security Knowledge-Bases

As we saw above, developers and QA, and even security teams, generally do not write their own security tests. Rather, products like HP's DevInspect, QAInspect, WebInspect, and AMP offer pre-packaged web application security expertise. Clearly, any security product is only as good as the security scans and tests it is able to execute, and this depends heavily on how knowledge of the latest attacks and threats are captured and encapsulated into security expertise that the products can use. These products must be infused with the most up-to-date and comprehensive security vulnerability database.

Users of HP's security solutions leverage SecureBase, a leading knowledgebase of application security vulncrabilities and best practices for fixing them. HP security experts find and capture known security vulnerabilities into the knowledgebase and constantly research the next generation of web application threats. As a result, users can download new vulnerability tests and description updates daily through the SmartUpdate feature (Figure 42).

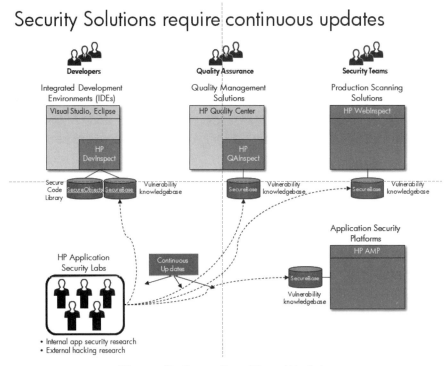

Figure 42: SecureBase/SmartUpdate

The final piece of the technology puzzle goes directly to the question of fitting into the existing landscape and operational processes. Fortunately, it's possible to find a solution that fits, and we can learn many lessons from how other thorny application lifecycle challenges around quality and performance have been solved.

Any technology that places an undue burden on its users or requires wholesale change is bound to fail. The best solutions are those that cause minimal disruption but provide great advantage over security threats. We strongly recommend that any application security product work directly within and with the development and QA solutions already in place. HP has built its security solutions with that design principle squarely in mind (see Appendix B).

So Where Does That Leave Us?

Application security has risen quickly to the top of the priority list for technology and business executives. It's a technical problem rooted in the fundamental architecture and intent of web applications. And as bad as it is today with Web 1.0 applications, the trends of Web 2.0 are making it worse.

> **Security vulnerabilities lie within the applications and are introduced through the development process.**

No matter the industry, application security risks and the consequences of a security breach are enormous and growing for nearly every enterprise. Unfortunately, as we have seen, no one security solution can be applied after the fact to solve this problem.

Organizations must take the problem seriously, by getting commitment up and down and across the organization to address the application security challenges. And they must understand the lifecycle nature of the problem and the need for a systemic, lifecycle solution approach.

> **Every enterprise can solve this problem.**

While a lifecycle approach with its many elements can seem daunting, each element is very do-able and can fit into the existing IT and operational landscape. Thus, many enterprises have implemented extremely successful application security and risk mitigation approaches.

Even though application security is a relatively new problem in the broader world of security, expertise and advanced technology are available from world-class providers like Hewlett Packard when an enterprise needs help.

Chapter 8

Test Sourcing: How Outsourcing Improves Cost Effective Testing

Outsourcing has been a part of IT since the 1980s. The IT environment was then typically handled by a single outsourcing partner. The result of that model was cost reduction and focus on core business competencies.

In the next-generation outsourcing model widely used today, an organization typically uses several partners that provide IT solutions for the business. Key benefits are transformation of the IT architecture and the alignment of business needs with IT.

> According to Dun & Bradstreet, 20 to 25 percent of IT outsourcing projects fail within two years, and 50 percent fail within five years.

If we compare the failure rate report to the results from the Standish Group (reported in Chapter 1) detailing why IT projects succeed, this finding is no surprise.

Dun & Bradstreet identified the following top reasons for failure:

- Inability of the organization commissioning outsourced work to articulate its needs (poor requirements definition)
- Inadequate vendor selection and contracting processes
- Inadequate supplier oversight
- Inadequate enterprise architecture and standards for vendor services and deliverables
- Inadequate management on the part of the acquirer

If an organization does not have well-defined processes, and the collaboration between the end-user group and IT is not working well, adding outsourcing or an external group to the equation does not improve the situation.

> Replacing internal IT personnel with low-cost resources from an external partner reduces costs for personnel, but does not improve the value for the end user.

Why — and How — Does Outsourcing Work in Other Industries?

In the infancy of the automobile industry, there was no such thing as an assembly line or any kind of automation. The growth and maturation of the auto industry gives us a good idea why the maturity of a process is important in order for outsourcing to work successfully.

Let's break down the evolution of car manufacturing to see how it reached the point where outsourcing could be a successful part of it.

In 1894, the Honorable Evelyn Henry Ellis decided to buy a car. Car dealers did not exist, so he went to Paris and commissioned a car from the well-known machine-tool company Panhard et Levassor. The automobile was produced using a classic handcraft model: Panhard and Levassor determined the exact specification for the car, ordered the necessary parts from different vendors, and assembled the final product.

The accuracy of the various parts in relation to the specification was approximate, given the lack of precise manufacturing technologies.

- During the final car assembly, which took place in a great hall, very skilled craftsmen assembled the car piece by piece, making adjustments to individual parts so everything fit together.

- When the car was finished, Ellis and a mechanic tested the car on the streets of Paris.

- After the car worked to his satisfaction, most likely after several adjustments in the assembly hall, Ellis set off in 1895 for England and became the first person to drive a car there.

18 years later, Henry Ford started an assembly line in Highland Park, Michigan, and manufactured cars at a fraction of the costs Panhard and Levassor incurred. The assembly line worked because:

- New technologies enabled accurate parts to be built.

- Ford introduced standards that allowed the pieces to fit together, with less time spent on adjustments.

- Workers stood at a belt and all the parts came to them for a single integration step.

The system Ford introduced drove the car industry for more than a century and was adopted all over the world. To increase efficiency and reduce production downtime, his company produced all the parts. Ford had total vertical integration, which allowed him to operate independently and control the quality and accuracy of every part used to build his cars. However, the system had some disadvantages:

- Models were limited by the uniformity necessary for low production costs.

- Administration costs were high.

- Quality of the end product varied, but technical problems with cars were common and customers were used to living with flaws.

Sixty years after Henry Ford introduced the assembly belt, another fundamental change occurred. At the Toyota factory in Japan, the engineer Taiichi Ohno was charged with producing a few thousand vehicles for the Japanese market.

He looked at the mass production systems in the United States and identified deficiencies, which he eliminated in a new production model. The result is a flexible system that:

- Achieves the efficiency of mass-production, but individualizes the product

- Eliminates the waste in the original mass production process

- Improves the process maturity in such a way that large parts of the production can be done by external vendors

To achieve this, Ohno came up with a new approach, which we know today as "lean production." The new system, used today by all successful car manufacturers, combines the advantages of the craftsmanship from the earliest car manufacturing process with the cost benefits and efficiency of a mass production system.

Ohno paved the way for successful outsourcing in the car manufacturing industry. The level of vertical integration in the industry today is between 25 and 30 percent, so almost two-thirds of the work building a car is done by external vendors, and the quality of the end product is higher than it ever has been in the history of the industry.

Successful IT Outsourcing

If we look at the auto industry's track record for successful outsourcing, it's clear that IT processes must be designed specifically to ensure that kind of success in outsourcing. The process needs to be repeatable enough to be able to hand off parts of it — it needs to be "mature."

IT processes have a lifecycle, and testing is part of that lifecycle. If you want to outsource any part of the process, it needs to be set up to accommodate the introduction of external vendors.

To use our car manufacturing example to illustrate, you might outsource parts of the process to companies that specialize in painting or chrome work. Auto painting companies can coat the cars better and more cheaply than you can. But if an external vendor is responsible for painting, you have to take the car out of the production line and the process you've established has to bring it back into the line smoothly.

If you're outsourcing to lower costs, you must be well-organized so you don't lose the cost benefit in managing the outsourcing. The maturity of the process can make or break your effort.

These days, the third generation of outsourcing focuses on increasing IT's business value and reducing applications' total cost of ownership. The key success factor is the "maturity" of the software products lifecycle — outsourcing does not improve the process, but it will fail if the processes are not mature.

To help companies assess the maturity of their processes, Hewlett Packard is collaborating with the Software Engineering Institute (SEI) to develop a process model based on the Capability Maturity Model Integration (CMMI). It's called CMMI-ACQ.[1]

1.See http://www.sei.cmu.edu/publications/documents/06.reports/06sr005.html.

In testing, we also need to consider the maturity of the test processes so test outsourcing is an option. Chapter 10 describes the process you need to observe when looking at the maturity of the software test lifecycle. We have to be sure we have unambiguous acceptance criteria, derived from the change request or requirement.

Let's look at why outsourcing all test activities doesn't make sense, and which activities can be outsourced successfully (Figure 43).

Phases of the test process

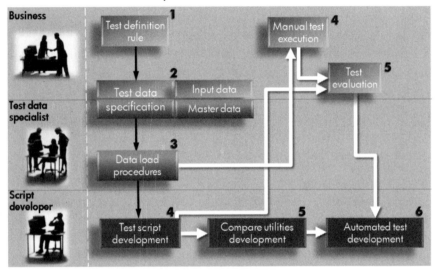

Figure 43: Phases of the test process

When we examine the various actions that need to happen in the course of testing, and the stakeholders involved, the tasks that can be outsourced are easy to identify.

Step 1: Test Rule Definition

This step has to do with communication and gathering information. It can be done by a test professional, but it has to be conducted onsite and in the local language, because most business end users are not comfortable speaking a foreign language. We intend to get information missing in the requirements, so reading between the lines and asking the right questions is key for the testing professional's success.

Step 2: Test Data Specification

This step has two elements: the input data and the master data. The input data description has to come from the business users, or at least be reviewed by them, whereas the master data can be taken care of by someone familiar with databases (the test data specialist), who can be external. The master data must be loaded into the system to match the input data in order to have a successful test execution.

Step 3: Data Load Procedures

This step is pure programming: It includes the load procedures for the database and the creation of stubs to simulate interfaces. The task requires knowledge of the system design, and can be obtained from the development team. It can be done competently by someone external or offsite, providing he has access to the system to be tested.

Step 4: Test Script Development

This step is only needed for test cases that will be automated. The input is the test-case description and the test-data specification. The work can be done remotely, providing the test script designer has access to the system under test or the development environment.

Step 5: Compare Utility Development

Compare utilities are software programs that help automatically compare the results of two test runs. The applications speed up the test evaluation process and reduce the likelihood of errors in this phase. Someone with programming and basic testing skills can build these utilities.

Step 6: Automated Test Evaluation

Along with scripts and the compare utilities, we usually require a set of programs that drive the whole test factory: loading the test data, starting the execution of the test scripts, saving the test results, running the compare utilities, saving the compare results, and finally informing the tester to check the compare results. This work can be completely outsourced with the necessary access to the environment.

Step 7: Manual Test Execution

In all cases where test cases are not automated, the test execution has to happen manually, usually by people with a business background. In any case, tight documentation of the expected results is important — if that's available, this step can be outsourced, providing the tester understands the language on the screen.

Step 8: Test Evaluation

The evaluation of test results must involve real people who will be end users — ultimately they're the only ones who can decide whether an application will work for their department. So, even when the whole process is automated, someone has to make this final check. In an ideal situation, the end user only has to check whether the test activities were executed properly and completely.

An overview the whole process shows us that a fair portion of the work can be outsourced (Figure 44).

Phases of the test process

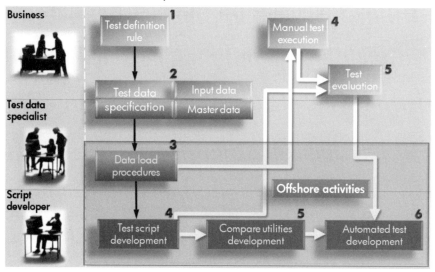

Figure 44: Potential for outsourcing

We've identified the activities that can be outsourced success-fully, but we've called on our experience with many such projects to develop a model that ensures successful completion of the project. You can use this to make sure the various people involved in your project are working effectively together and the project is properly managed (Figure 45).

Testing center

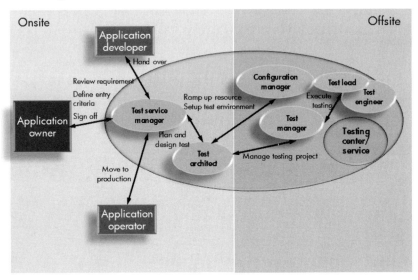

Figure 45: Testing center roles

The onsite team usually consists of local people, or at least people with local language skills. This is mainly to make sure that another communication challenge is not introduced. The onsite people are leading all the different activities. Over time, the proportion of work that needs to be done onsite will be reduced, compared to the work that can come from offsite. Maintenance of the automated test cases can be handled offsite, provided there are no significant changes in the functionality of the software.

Along with the processes that need to be in place, the qualification of those who work with the outsourcing partners is important. Because support should go beyond test automation and execution, a tool certification is not enough — a standard has been developed to educate testers. (The syllabus for the Foundation Level and the Advanced Level certification can be downloaded from http://www.istqb.org/download.htm.)

> When you select a partner for outsourcing,
> formal certification is a good differentiator.

Last, but definitely not least, make sure the organization you choose to work with has a sound approach and system that can be adapted to the processes your organization uses.

Chapter 9

SUCCESSFUL Goal-Driven KPI Approach

*"Count what is countable, measure what is measurable,
and what is not measurable, make measurable."*
- Galileo, (1564-1642)

In the previous chapters, we've presented a formalized and practical approach to software testing. We want it to be easy to understand, but more importantly, easy to implement.

Many in the industry today still see testing processes as fluff created by business consultants or universities to add overhead and paperwork to already over-burdened staff. Testing processes *can* be very rigorous, and they take dedication and time to prove their value. And busy managers may neglect to

191

measure progress or track test results to determine if the adopted testing process adds enough value for the effort it takes.

Without seeing real successes, many organizations abandon their formalized testing processes.

> Blindly following and implementing testing processes has been the downfall of many quality initiatives.

The good news is that many companies are implementing quality metrics to give management more visibility into their quality initiatives in order to help them make business decisions.

The biggest challenge to this initiative is determining what to measure and what *key performance indicators (KPIs)* to use. A KPI is a quantifiable metric applied over a period of time to measure an organization's current status and progress in achieving its business goals.

Because this book aims to align testing with business outcomes, we want to determine if the testing process the business adopts (whether the HP Quality Model or another) really contributes to the improvement of these business objectives. We also want to see if adopting these testing processes allows organizations to continuously improve on their testing efficiency and effectiveness.

But what do we measure? What KPIs should we use to help us make this determination?

In this chapter, we present a simple goal-driven, top-down approach to determine what to measure and what metrics to use, based on the business objectives and business goals (Figure 46).

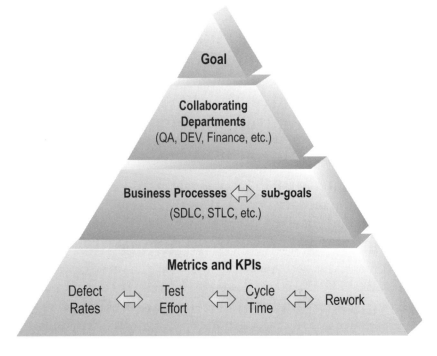

Figure 46: A goal-driven, top-down KPI approach

Business goals should determine what to measure and what KPIs to use. After all, if the KPIs aren't aligned with what the business is set up to achieve, why bother to track those KPIs at all?

Organizations are sometimes confused when tasked with creating a report or dashboard for a specific goal. Everyone has ideas and suggestions of what metrics to use and the conversation often becomes a very technical one. This leads to creating metrics that can't be interpreted or turn out not to be useful in addressing the business questions at hand.

Don't ask, "What types of metrics should I use?" Instead, focus on what you really need to learn or understand about the business.

> One of the axioms of metrics is: What gets measured gets done. So ask, "What do we want done?"

When you fully understand what you need to learn or understand about the business and what factors directly affect the business, figuring out what to measure and what KPIs to use will become more apparent.

Many organizations fail to involve all the departments when they design the metrics. If each department that affects the business goal is not engaged in the process, the measurements can be inaccurate. Why? Because data is probably missing.

Even worse, if the various departments can't agree on measurements, we can't compare the results from those departments, and it becomes more difficult to make sense of what we're measuring because we're no longer comparing apples to apples.

Here are a few items that should be considered in setting up KPIs:

- The technical staff needs to be involved to determine the best ways to gather and process the data that make up the KPIs.

- A normalization and collaboration process has to take place so all departments agree on the KPIs and use the same language and definition for the values of the KPIs.

- Think about what to do after you have obtained the values of the KPIs. Having KPIs and values without an action plan to execute on them is like knowing all the scores of every sporting event in the future and not having a plan to make a bet.

Okay, now we reveal why we shouted *SUCCESSFUL* at you in the title of this chapter — it spells out the 10 steps of our goal-driven approach to a successful testing endeavor (Figure 47). These steps come from years of experience and the following formula will set you on the right course for getting the full benefit of your testing efforts:

1. **S**et business goals.

2. **U**nderstand the impact of departments on those business goals.

3. **C**hoose supporting business processes.

4. **C**reate business-process goals.

5. **E**xamine what to measure.

6. **S**tandardize measurements across departments.

7. **S**cope data source and integration needs.

8. **F**ormalize indicators and thresholds.

9. **U**tilize and execute appropriate action plans.

10. **L**ay the groundwork and baseline.

This is an iterative process. Revisit these steps regularly because business goals may change. Or you may discover that the metrics you've chosen are not delivering exactly what you wanted.

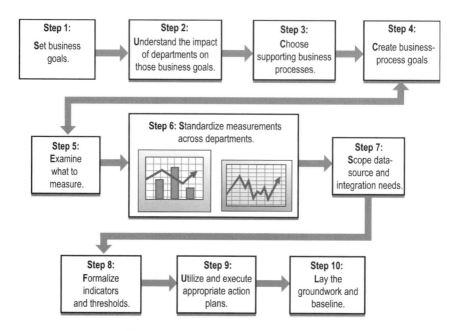

Figure 47: The 10 SUCCESSFUL steps

Set Business Goals

The first step in our approach should be fairly self explanatory. One can argue that you can never achieve anything without setting goals, because you wouldn't know when you have achieved them. This approach is predicated on setting appropriate business goals.

The purpose of understanding KPIs and creating dashboards and reports to give visibility is to help us make better decisions toward satisfying our business goals.

> Business goals are high-level goals that affect an entire organization or company.

Every organization has such goals — cutting the cost of running the business or getting products to market faster. Every individual in the organization or company is striving toward these goals.

It's important to note that we use the term business *goals* and not business *objectives*. These terms are often used interchangeably in the industry.

From our perspective, business objectives are determined first — the need to cut IT cost, the need to improve customer service, etc.

Business goals are typically derived from those business objectives, but the key difference is that we can quantify the goals — they have to be measurable. For example, a business goal is to cut IT costs by 20 percent. Or, we have to improve customer satisfaction ratings on a scale of 1–10 by two points.

> How can you determine if you've achieved your business *objectives* without some way to quantify whether you're reaching your business *goals*?

Typically, these business goals are set by the heads of the organizations with input from their direct reports so the goals are reachable.

The number of high-level business goals is typically few — around three or so — as most organizational heads want resources to be targeted in key areas. Having too many goals at one time can only add confusion and make each individual goal difficult to achieve.

It's helpful to ask questions around the business goals to better understand them — the answers will be useful later when determining indicator thresholds. Ask what the internal goals are, versus external goals. Perhaps the sales target internally is $2 million dollars, while the target set externally is only $1.8 million dollars.

Many organizations set a higher internal goal than their external goal, so even a slight shortfall of the internal goal will still allow them to make their external goals, which makes their stakeholders or investors happy.

Also ask questions that help you determine milestones or checkpoints so if progress falls behind, your teams can agree on action plans to catch up. Or in some cases, reality checks may lead you to redefine success in order to make the business goal more achievable.

Understand the Impact of Each Department on Business Goals

Okay, after business goals have been set and we've investigated the goals thoroughly, we need to focus on the departments that should collaborate on achieving the goals.

> **Identify which departments have direct and indirect impacts on a particular goal and you'll make the best business decisions.**

Using the business goal of cutting IT costs by 20 percent, we consider various IT departments that could contribute to that cost cutting. Departments that directly impact this goal may include the development team, the QA team, the operations team, the support team, and off-shore teams. Reallocating the resources and budgets of these teams can have a direct effect in the cost of IT.

Indirectly, we may want to consider the demand non-IT departments are putting on the IT teams. For example, a line of business may want to offer an additional service to its customers immediately; however, the internal IT cost of providing this service is astronomical.

By re-evaluating this idea, and perhaps outsourcing the implementation of the service to a business partner or delaying the implementation, we can indirectly reduce the pressure put on the IT organization and thereby reduce IT costs (Figure 48).

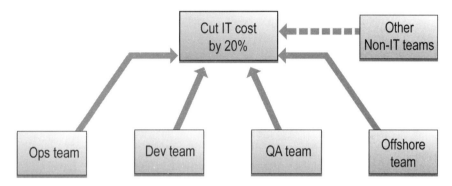

Figure 48: Sample departments that might impact the cost-cutting goal

Choose Supporting Business Processes

Now, for each department that has direct or indirect impacts on the business goal, we must isolate the business processes that could contribute to the business goal. To cut IT costs, we may want to look at the software development lifecycle (SDLC) of the development team to discover if changes can make the SDLC more efficient. In the QA team, we might see if we can improve the effectiveness of the testing process or make the defect process more efficient.

> Evaluate the various attributes of each business process that affects IT costs, such as staff, software, hardware, training, and so on.

By starting with the business processes, we'll see where to streamline those processes before examining the business model attributes to determine the action that allows us to best achieve the business goal (Figure 49).

> This approach allows us to take a step back and strategize at a higher level and consider the overall business model before making tactical decisions.

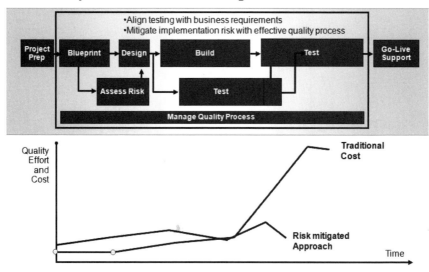

A Sample Streamlined Testing Process

Figure 49: A sample risk mitigated-testing process that may help cut IT costs

Create Business Process Goals

Business process goals are subgoals derived from the business processes described in the last section. They should also align with the business goal.

The logic is that setting cost-cutting goals for a business process within the departments and aligning them with the original business goal of cutting IT costs by 20%, we can be confident that the business process goals are also aligned with the business goals.

> Limit these goals to just a few so you get a clear picture of what you're trying to learn and they're not too hard to track or interpret.

Let's continue with the example of trying to cut IT costs by 20 percent. Using the testing process from the QA team, we can derive a simple process goal to cut the total testing cost by 20 percent.

We can also create subgoals of this process goal. One might be to increase test efficiency by 20 percent. Another subgoal could be to create a strategy to determine if outsourcing can help lower testing resource costs by 20 percent.

Examine What to Measure

Keep three things in mind when you examine what to measure. The first is a quote from Albert Einstein, one of the smartest people we know of.

1. "Everything that can be counted does not necessarily count; everything that counts cannot necessarily be counted." - *Albert Einstein*

There will always be intangible elements that cannot be counted. And we can count some items that are not aligned with the business goal, but they're probably not important to us. That brings us to the second point.

2. Continue to ask why we measure, and take the accuracy of what you are measuring seriously.

Because we're aligning with business goals and these business goals are what all individuals within an organization are striving for, simply remember that what gets measured gets done. Work done that is not measured often leads to rework or redundancies.

3. Start with a list of quantifiable questions to ask for each subgoal.

We find it's much easier to figure out what metrics to use or what to measure when we ask the right questions — of the right people.

Interviewing those responsible for the subgoals within a department is a good tactic. Also, talk to the people who are familiar with the relevant business process. Ask questions related to the attributes of the business process subgoal.

If our subgoal is to determine a strategy for outsourcing that can lower testing resource costs, we might consider asking questions such as:

- What is the cost ratio between outsourcers and internal resources?

- What is the productivity level of the outsourcers?

- To cut testing costs by 20 percent, how much should we outsource in order to keep the same level of overall productivity?

Based on the answer to these questions, we might then create a strategy to determine how much we can afford to outsource by weighting factors of business/management viability ratings, productivity, and overall internal satisfaction with outsourcers.

We then calculate each of these high-level metrics and support them through a predetermined formula by a set of lower-level metrics. A way to look at productivity is to simply compare the productivity of outsourcers to internal employees, and then correlate that to the cost ratio to determine the ROI of outsourcing.

For example, for the testing-resource outsourcing-productivity metric, the lower-level metrics in Table 6 could help calculate and support the productivity metric.

Metric	Measurement Description	Standard Value
Rejected defects	Measures the time wasted by Development and QA as a result of false defects to improve the ability of QA engineers to identify and report defects	< 5%
Reopen defects	Measures the effectiveness of the bug-fixing process and QA within this process	< 5%
Defect detection time effectiveness	Measures the speed with which QA detects major defects	>50%
Defect-fix ratio	Measures the percentage of defects found and fixed by Development, out of the total defects found by testers	TBD
Regression defects	Measures the type of work outcome and the type of tasks	TBD
Testing design quantity and pro-duction	Checks the type of and the effectiveness of tests (number of defects found by the tests)	TBD

Table 6: Sample set of lower-level metric used to determined outsourced testing productivity

Standardize Measurements Across Departments

Although we determine metrics by using the business process subgoals and aligning them with various departments, it's important to use the same metrics across departments when there are similar subgoals. Many times, departments work in silos and either create different sets of metrics for the same sub-goal or use different values to represent the same metric.

In the productivity example above, one QA team may use a set of metrics and values, but another QA team that does some outsourcing may come up with a completely different set of metrics or have different standard values of measurements.

> The problem is not the differences themselves, but interpretation of the results of these metrics.

We could not compare the productivity ratings of the two departments unless they collaborate on a metric-value normalization process that can equate different values from different departments.

In the above example, we may consider using a *defect rejection ratio* instead of the number of *rejected defects* so we can compare this metric from two different QA teams working on two different projects.

In some situations, a more meaningful comparison may be to have one project with 20 *regression defects* and fewer total defects weigh the same as another project with 50 *regression defects* and more total defects.

> The idea is to find ways to interpret data with accuracy and be able to properly compare data across departments.

This step will also help you get agreement between departments on what's important to measure and help teams agree on the metrics and the interpretations of these metrics.

Scope Data Source and Integration Needs

At this point, we've determined the metrics and documented them. We've standardized and gained agreement across organizations.

Now we need to determine the data source of the metrics and if any data needs to be integrated to produce the reports and the dashboard views we need for evaluating them.

We might determine that the outsourcing-financial data will come from an enterprise resource planning (ERP) system, the testing data will come from the HP Quality Center platform, and other IT governance data will come from HP PPM Center software project and portfolio modules.

> Always weigh the feasibility and ease of getting the data when creating metrics and allocate enough resources and time to set up the technology required to capture the data you want.

Formalize Indicators and Thresholds

Simply having the right metrics and data that map to the goals isn't enough. You must have a set of rules or indicators to help you interpret the data.

The rules used to interpret the data are data thresholds, which should allow you to easily understand the data and to make business decisions.

> Data thresholds must be agreed upon so anyone looking at the data will interpret it the same way.

Using the productivity example again, we might set thresholds at 90 percent and 70 percent. So, if the outsourcer's productivity is 90 percent and above, compared to the internal resources, we determine that to be *great* and associate the number with a green indicator. If the outsourcer's productivity is between 70 and 90 percent, then we consider this a *warning* status and associate the number with a yellow indicator. If the outsourcer's productivity is below 70 percent, we consider this a *failure* and associate it with a red indicator.

These thresholds help us generate the reports and the dashboard views that management can understand (Figure 50).

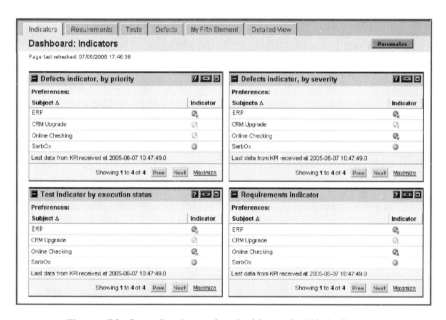

Figure 50: Sample view of a dashboard with indicators

Many people confuse reports and dashboards. Often, dashboard tools are used as reporting tools and vice versa. Let's discuss the differences and reduce the confusion.

A *dashboard* provides up-to-date dynamic snapshots or indicators of the current state of the business, which allows an individual to make fast business decisions.

A *report* tells a more detailed story and discusses the process of how the business got to its current state.

A good example of dashboard indicators is what happens when you check stock prices. The vicissitudes of dynamic stock pricing allow you make quick decisions about selling or buying the stock. You may also set thresholds to automatically sell or buy the stock, based on this information.

A report, in this instance, might be the financial report of the same stock that discusses the business conditions for the past year, the detailed process of how the business was run and perhaps the market condition that influenced the price of the stock. This is a more detailed secondary analysis to help you understand the stock, after you determine from the indicator that something is either very good or very bad about the stock.

Trying to provide every bit of data or metric possible in a dashboard or report creates clutter that makes it difficult to find the data you need to see.

Including too much information makes it harder to implement reporting, and it often causes problems with systems that host the dashboard and/or reports.

Utilize and Execute Appropriate Action Plans

All the preparation to determine the KPIs and thresholds aligned with the business goal comes down to the action plans associated with them.

> Be prepared to act, based on the predefined thresholds.

Can you imagine learning all the probabilities and statistics of poker and then not having an action plan to either bid or fold when the appropriate pot odds appear? You would have wasted your effort collecting all that data.

> An action plan is a series of tasks or decisions to follow or make when a certain threshold level is reached.

In Figure 51, we determine that if the outsourcing indicator is green, we should look into outsourcing more in order to cut testing resource costs. If the outsourcing indicator is yellow, we would maintain the status quo. But if the outsourcing indicator is red, we would start to decrease outsourcing and replace outside contractors with more internal resources. Note: in this book, the colors green, yellow, red will show up as gray, white, and black.

Always associate action plans with indicators and be ready to execute your plans immediately to respond to the dynamic changes of today's business environment.

Outsourcer Productivity

Team's Productivity bottom line	July
Integrations	102%
CRM	93%
AR Module	96%
AP Module	94%
Time tracking	82%
Billing	79%
Regression	60%
In-source team	100%

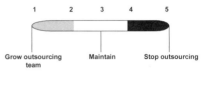

Figure 51: Sample outsourcing indicator with actions

Lay the Groundwork and Baseline

Remember we mentioned continuous improvement earlier? The only way to see that continuous improvement is to have a good understanding of the initial state of the business, and periodically compare the original state to the current state.

> Take a snapshot of the initial state of the business and use this data as the baseline of comparison during a time in the future.

The first nine steps of this approach have helped us determine all the items we need for the implementation. In this final step, we simply implement the KPIs through standard reports and dashboards, then we compare the snapshots of the business now with where we started.

In summary, the *SUCCESSFUL* goal-driven KPI approach is a logical and simple series of steps to follow to create a measurement strategy.

The 10-step process we've outlined is an iterative process — every time a business goal is reached, we need to revisit these

10 steps to set new goals and determine which items to modify to realign with the new business goals.

We have now introduced our entire software testing approach based on our experiences and the HP Software Quality Model. In the next chapter, we bring the concepts of this book together and help you understand how to start implementing our practical approach to software testing.

Chapter 10

Getting Started: Putting It All Together

The first rule of any technology used in a business is that automation applied to an efficient operation will magnify the efficiency. The second is that automation applied to an inefficient operation will magnify the inefficiency.
-Bill Gates

We have discussed many things so far, and now it's time to put them all together in a way that will help you with your projects. Let's consider two different situations.

The first occurs at the beginning of a project when you're planning how you'll create, test, and deploy some new application or changes to an existing application. The second situation is, unfortunately, more common: you're in the middle of the test, things are not going as planned, and the deadline is looming. Now what?

Because you're probably in the second situation (and that's probably why you're reading this book), let's talk about that one. Instead of doing everything we've talked about so far, you only have time for a subset, so what should you do?

1. **Structure the application from a business point of view.** Divide it into main processes, subprocesses, and

business functions, and link the requirements with the business functions.

2. **Prioritize the business functions.** In the time you have left, concentrate on the important things. You probably won't have time to test all the requirements, so this involves decisions to withdraw or deploy requirements. These are risk decisions, and the answers will be different for different requirements.

    Earlier testing may have already addressed some of these requirements, and that information will be useful in your decisions. (It's important to inform the business stakeholders at this point which requirements you're not going to test.)

3. **Define the test rules.** Use equivalence partitioning for the most critical business functions.

4. **Complete the test rules.** Add data and organizational details to executable test cases.

5. **Link all test cases to the requirements.** Do this for the new test cases you create based on the behavioral models, as well as for all the existing test cases you're running or plan to run.

    The reasons for doing this are twofold. It allows us to make sure we're testing the high-priority business functions. It also reduces the number of test cases that may be necessary to complete the remaining schedule, and you don't want to drop any test cases that are actually helping to meet the objectives. If you can't link a test case to a requirement, consider dropping that test case.

6. **Link any defects found to test cases and requirements.** When everything is connected to everything in this way, we increase visibility and therefore improve project management.

7. **Report on requirement status.** Just as when you link defects to requirements, this type of reporting increases visibility and improves project management.

8. **Leverage prebuilt testing assets.** Finally, if you are in the middle of creating test cases or perhaps attempting to automate enterprise resource planning (ERP) applications, you can leverage some significant prebuilt testing assets and increase your testing efficiency by up to 300 percent from manual testing.

Now let's examine the situation where you have a bit more time for an in-depth approach. In other words, while the preceding situation tells you what to do when you're *heading* for trouble, here we'll assume you have the time to prevent trouble.

To be successful in your quality initiatives, consider all the elements of what we call the "quality ecosystem." These elements have to do with the governance and the testing itself:

- Requirements
- Reporting
- Defect management
- Performance-issue management
- Shared services
- Test environment
- Test planning and design
- Key performance indicators (KPIs)
- Unit testing
- Integration testing
- System testing
- Performance testing
- User acceptance testing
- Operational readiness

You may want to modify this list to match the terminology in your organization. There are many ways of referring to these quality elements, especially when it comes to naming the various stages of the software testing lifecycle (STLC).

The first step is to figure out what changes you need to make. Then determine where you are today. This will establish a baseline against which you can measure progress. We use the HP Software Quality Continuum to help determine the current state of an organization.

As a guide to quality and process improvement, the HP Software Quality Continuum defines quality-related characteristics on a progressive scale. The purpose of the HP Software Quality Continuum is to provide a scale for the baseline of an organization's status — how does it line up with the elements of the quality ecosystem? Locating an organization along the HP Software Quality Continuum is the first step in determining where to make investments in quality improvement.

The scale is divided into five levels from Level 0 (quality agnostic) through Level 4 (quality expert).

Level 0: Quality Agnostic

The quality agnostic organization is one in which quality is not considered in any processes. There is little or no recognition of the opportunities available or the cost associated with the lack of quality in the products or processes.

This does not mean that Level 0 companies cannot produce articles of value; many software organizations start off this way and mature as time goes by.

> Level 0 organizations are typically quite small with a close-knit staff in constant communication with each other.

Level 1: Quality Initializing

A quality initializing organization often conducts all quality activities and processes with its development and IT personnel who wear multiple hats.

A Level 1 group also performs tests to verify and validate the development, integration, configuration, design, and architecture infrastructure. Although this level generally has no formal QA processes to follow, it's important to recognize that Level 1 organizations can typically point to case studies or independent instances within the organization that indicate a higher level of maturity.

While some groups within a Level 1 organization may follow processes or possess technology that may be arguably more aligned with a higher level, the ranking is based on the propagation of these advantages so they achieve enterprise-wide efficiency and effectiveness. In cases with conflicting rationale (while most departments are more aligned with a Level 1, some departments are really at Level 2), this can guide the progression to Level 2 using hands-on examples within the same organization.

> **Level 1 organizations are typically medium to large in size and are reactive to quality problems.**

They often rely on individual expertise rather than repeatable process. These companies have recognized the drawbacks of this ad hoc approach and they're developing process improvements and introducing software products to automate their improved processes. They're also exploring organizational changes to improve quality.

Process Characteristics:

- They do not outline or document the requirements-gathering process.

- They send requirements directly to the project manager.
- The organization has no formal review process — they do not review formal requirements or testing.
- Test plans do not cover all the test types.
- They do not evaluate dependencies and business risks.
- The performance optimization process is ad hoc and sporadic across projects and applications.
- Little or no performance reporting takes place.
- No functional- or component-testing guidelines exist.
- No defect-tracking process for the project takes place.
- They do not track or report standards metrics.

Product Characteristics:

- Software support products such as automated testing, version control, and demand management are either not in use or are used only in pockets in the organization.
- There is no shared repository or otherwise common location for the information and documentation relevant to the projects in the organization.

People Characteristics:

- Development leads write the majority of planning documents without consulting much with other teams.
- No dedicated quality-focused team exists.
- Developers create tests and are responsible for test-scenario execution.
- Project managers or development leads write test plans.

Level 2: Quality Conscious

The quality conscious organization is "personnel focused" — it relies heavily on individuals and personnel performance. Less weight is given to the technology or process because the quality conscious personnel are isolated from each other and little technology or process exists to help them collaborate.

At this level of the quality maturity scale, we'll likely find that personnel are pushed to their limits to compensate for the lack of technology or processes.

Level 2 organizations are professionally structured for quality assurance, in that quality — as a concept — is known, understood, and pursued by the enterprise. The organization recognizes the intrinsic value (return on investment, economies of scale) that quality mechanisms provide to the enterprise's business processes, and so it's beginning to establish a quality ecosystem.

At this stage, the quality ecosystem is mostly project-focused technologies and fundamental project processes, such as requirements-gathering and broad validation techniques. The quality ecosystem includes dedicated personnel (usually technical quality engineers) who deploy quality assurance practices. Project plans include testing activities, and test assets are documented and maintained in some form of repository.

A project QA team conducts testing and is responsible for enforcing quality processes and performance optimization, but no standard has been established. A defect-tracking process is implemented, although it's not part of a larger test-management software platform. Administrative efficiencies that can be realized through technologies are starting to become important, although the ecosystem has no processes to govern these tools.

The ecosystem is split and not cohesive on an enterprise scale, although pockets of efficiencies throughout the lines of businesses point to the possibility of shared technical services as the next logical step. Sharing personnel skill-set efficiencies, workflows, and technical assets from one line of business to another will be the driving force toward a move to Level 3, where the technology helps realize efficiencies.

> Level 2 organizations are typically medium to large companies that are highly federated, made up of disparate organizations or lines of business.

Process Characteristics:

- The organization has not outlined nor documented a requirements-gathering process on a consistent basis. Requirements are sent directly by business (or by a higher-level business process, such as "Sizing") to a project manager.

- Project managers or development leads write test plans, but they do not cover all the Performance Test types.

- The development lead writes the majority of planning documents without consulting much with other teams.

- Dependencies and business risks are not evaluated.

- Performance and functional testing activity processes are ad hoc and sporadic across projects and applications.

- The organization undertakes little or no performance testing. Performance metrics, reports, diagnostics, and environmental monitoring offer little value even when they are reported. Any performance-testing processes included in this phase are not necessarily in synch with functional testing.

- A formal quality process for all testing projects is established and in use. The process is project-based and is intended for short-term project-focused initiatives. (No portfolio initiatives exist organically within the quality ecosystem — the many project initiatives are disconnected from each other, but together serve the portfolio's objectives.)

■ A quality-review process is in place. Artifacts for the review are produced in a basic format and template. The review process focuses on technical specifications only, not business requirements.

■ Defect tracking is taking place, although visibility is limited to the project level — not across all projects — and visibility is not offered upstream to management.

■ Change-management processes are systematic and follow a known procedure, although not necessarily the same across each project. Control for the change-approval process is dispersed.

Product Characteristics:

■ Project-level, demand-management software is not in place that links to quality-assurance software, although manual processes exist to facilitate the movement of demand from request to test. For example, data-acquisition demand processes are manual by way of email or phone.

■ Version-control tools are leveraged for both documentation management and technical-asset management to some extent.

■ A shared repository is in place for storage of various types of business and technical assets. However, no linkage exists between these two types — the repository is not capable of doing this.

■ Basic automation has been introduced to the QA team and is implemented where possible. Complex tasks are not automated. Some tasks are left for manual operation, usually because of limited resources (budget limitations and lack of time needed to learn about the automation strategy or train for product adoption) and the lack of implementation experience.

- Efforts to integrate disparate software mechanisms for QA reporting, automation, and management needs are highly unreliable. Reporting software is not standardized across the enterprise, although some standard metrics have been identified.

- If any monitoring of the systems under test is taking place, it is manual.

- One or more reporting tools are in place. They convey status, but there is little integration with the quality-assurance software that produces the information. Linkage is manual at best, and logical correlation between the various reports is difficult or not possible.

- Change-management products do not exist or are not integrated with quality-assurance products. A consolidated and integrated approach is necessary to link the two domains and to facilitate the intended processes for work requests and shared services.

People Characteristics:

- A QA role has been formally designated. In many cases, however, the QA person has additional non-QA responsibilities, probably because of budget, and so is under some time pressures. Also many of these teams are not aware of the advantages of automation or test design, and so designating personnel to focus solely on quality assurance does not make sense to them.

- Personnel that complement work streams for QA (business analysts and technical administrators) have been formally designated to support this early stage of the quality ecosystem. There is a commitment to improve communication between business and technology with an effective layer of customer relationship management (CRM).

- A team leader or project manager conducts informal review processes. Reviews are internal only and oftentimes are ad hoc. Review processes seem to be more ideally structured and implemented in the CRM category.

- Support personnel are in place, but they usually take a delegation role. The team leader or project manager often plays this role at this level of maturity.

- Some QA personnel are formally trained on QA automation products in use; however, often no follow-up mentoring or hands-on consulting is available after training to complement the new knowledge. (This situation, combined with the lack of opportunity for the formal QA team to add value to projects, lengthens the adoption and optimization of automation technologies substantially.)

- No process training happens at this level — the processes are left to the users to learn separately.

- Requirements are created by business-level personnel and handed off to QA. The QA team has no feedback mechanism or influence on requirements.

Level 3: Quality Savvy

A company or organization is at the quality-savvy level if they have a dedicated team of QA personnel with expertise in implementation, configuration, maintenance, and support of quality test and monitoring products. This organization should have established official request-management processes to support the various organizational test teams.

A set of product best practices can be replicated consistently across several lines of business and test groups. The quality group acts as the central point of contact and support for all test and monitoring products. They assist and guide test teams in proper performance and product use and in validating the development, integration, configuration, and infrastructure builds per the design specifications.

Standardized data-gathering and reporting processes use automated test and monitoring product solutions.

Level 3 organizations are typically large, integrated companies with shared infrastructure and common processes. They are often financial, insurance, or medical institutions.

Process Characteristics:

- The organization has standard data-gathering and reporting processes.

- Best practices for software test and SDLCs have been documented.

- Automation guidelines and test-process best practices exist.

- QA uses known standards and collaborative workflows.

- Customer support for products is available.

- Charge back is based on centralized licenses, infrastructure, resources, and product-related service requests.

- Business-case and ROI analysis for products is in place.

- Demand-management processes are in place.

- Cross-project test management and performance-test reporting are in place.

- A center of excellence exists, with a shared, consulting-services framework and funding/charge-back options.

- The company has internal billing capabilities.

- A test lab infrastructure is operational.

- The organization implements risk mitigation, has established quality gates, and applies exit criteria before moving into the next phase of the SDLC.

- Service-level reporting is in place.

- Business-case templates and procedures have been developed.

- An internal marketing process exists for services shared across business units.

- A formal communication process is established between all teams.

- Testing services are provided across multiple lines of business.

Product Characteristics:

- Automated testing is in use throughout the organization.

- Product and test lab/infrastructure administration processes are in place.

- Demand management is enforced by HP PPM Center software product implementation.

- Standard data-gathering and reporting processes use automated test and application-monitoring product solutions.

- Automated test management and performance design is in place.

- A dashboard is implemented with real-time reporting capabilities and test metrics.

- Testing products test application components, business processes, and scenarios.

- A dashboard gives visibility into project status.

- Dashboard validation and certification services are performed.

People Characteristics:

- Management focuses on hiring experienced quality-focused technical personnel.

- Experts in test-management, performance-testing, and application-monitoring products are in place.

- Resources are scheduled for product customization, maintenance, and support.

- Training and certification is readily available for staff.

- QA has its own budget.

- QA is involved up front in the SDLC.

- QA estimates the number of hours it needs to complete a testing task and quality work.

- 24/7, enterprise-wide, testing-product infrastructure and support is in place.

Level 4: Quality Expert

An organization is at a quality expert level when it has formal quality processes, often enforced and supported by products, and dedicated product and process QA experts that can be leveraged across the organization. It emphasizes a continuous improvement of process best practices, and uses metrics to measure quality.

In addition, responsibilities of the centralized QA group include creation and certification of quality gate processes, training and mentoring of application test teams, and guidance of process and product implementation. Internal marketing practices are in place and service-level reporting is performed. The service utility may also be involved with or completely manage the performance optimization services, which would include infrastructure tuning (application testing, reliability, scalability, and stress tests).

It is usually the case that Level 4 organizations are thought leaders in best practices and methodology. Level 4 organizations typically have personnel with black belts in Six Sigma, and/or follow industry-standard quality procedures such as those found in ITIL.

The monetary cost of entry into the Level 4 domain is high, and it's the main consideration for most organizations. For instance, if the cost of moving from Level 3 to Level 4 is drastically higher than the benefit added to the quality ecosystem, there is understandably little rationale for investing in such an ambition.

> Level 4 organizations are completely driven by quality, and can only exist by employing strict quality standards that meet government-imposed or industry-imposed regulations or restrictions.

Process Characteristics:

- A formal communication process is established.

- Quality validation and certification services are performed.

- Metrics have been agreed upon and reporting at the centralized application level is obtained.

- Cross-project test management and performance-test reporting is done.

- Test automation training and mentoring capabilities are in place.

- Known standards and collaborative workflows govern the day-to-day activities of the organization. The organization cannot exist without complete adherence to these standards.

Product Characteristics:

- Automated service-level reporting (service level of the utility) is in place.

- An industry-standard quality model is used.

- All quality reviews, quality gates, and process reviews are standardized.

- Standardized services and metrics are based on best practices.

- A dashboard is in place that gives organization-wide visibility into the status of all projects.

- IT governance solutions digitize most quality ecosystem workflows.

People Characteristics:

- Advanced test engineering personnel provide testing services across multiple lines of businesses.

- Functional test organization and automation expertise is reviewed by certified industry standards organizations. Functional and/or performance testing is always completed to government or industry specifications.

- Project/test management expertise is typically in line with Project Management Office-based structures such as the Project Management Institute.

- Certified industry personnel act as quality managers. Quantified experience and structured certification-based training is mandatory to achieve this level.

Self Evaluation – Designing a Roadmap

When we work with client organizations to help with quality improvement, we first determine their current level, develop a set of recommendations, and design a roadmap for implementing the recommendations. Our process looks like Figure 52.

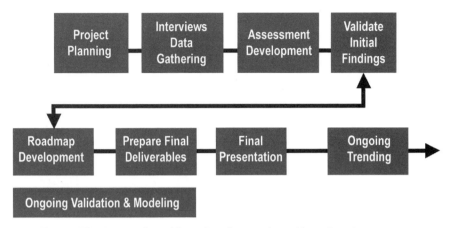

Figure 52: A sample self evaluation and quality planning process

To put this in context for you, most of the organizations we see start off in the mid-Level 1 to mid-Level 2 range.

When you start applying the concepts, practices, and recommendations in this book, it is useful to approach a transition from where you are with two perspectives in mind — strategic and tactical.

The strategic approach is to decide where you want the organization to go. Do you want to be at Level 4? Is Level 2 good enough to serve your business goals? These are business decisions. Any advance in quality is an investment, and you must consider the amount to be invested and your organization's tolerance for change.

After you decide on your target level, it is necessary to determine where you are today. If you're already operating at the level that suits your business goals, declare victory and move on. Most of us, however, have room for improvement.

To determine where you are today, review the quality continuum above. Be very objective in comparing your organization to the descriptions of each level. This comparison will show you areas you can and should improve, and your efforts should focus on those areas.

> Tactically, one of the biggest inhibitors to quality is the all-too-common lack of communication between IT and the business.

More than just getting the requirements agreed upon, business stakeholders and IT need to be in communication throughout the project. IT will want business input for review and test-plan approval. The business will need to understand progress and trends as the IT work continues, so managers can prepare for the changes coming to the software or systems.

This means that establishing a governing body or committee made up of both IT and business stakeholders is very important for the success of any project. The frequency of communication should depend on the risks associated with the project and its current status.

Let's summarize our strategy and tactics:

> Strategy
> - Determine where you are and where you want to be.
> - Align quality initiatives to business outcomes.
>
> Tactics
> - Build a communication mechanism between IT and business.
> - Implement the changes suggested by your strategic review.

While we are now at the end of the book, this is just the beginning for you. The things we've discussed in this and previous chapters are all a part of what makes a test — and a project — successful. Good luck, and have fun.

Common Test Techniques

In Chapter 1, we described test phases and why they are important. All of the test phases fall into two basic test types, white-box testing and black-box testing. The following lists common test techniques used for each test type.

White-Box Testing Techniques

The seven most common techniques and approaches of white-box testing are described here.

Syntax Testing

ANALYSIS: Syntax testing uses a model of the formally defined syntax of the inputs to a component. We represent the syntax as a number of rules, each of which defines the possible means of production of a symbol in terms of sequences of, iterations of, or selections between other symbols.

DESIGN: We design test cases with valid and invalid syntax from the formally defined syntax of the inputs to the component. Test cases with valid syntax are intended to execute options derived from the following rules (although additional rules may apply):

- Whenever a selection is used, an option is derived for each alternative by replacing the selection with that alternative.

- Whenever an iteration is used, at least two options are derived: one with the minimum number of iterated symbols, and the other with more than the minimum number of repetitions.

A test case may exercise any number of options.

For each test case, specify the following items:

- Input(s) to the component
- Option(s) exercised
- Expected outcome of the test case

Test cases with invalid syntax are designed as follows:

- Document a checklist of generic mutations that can be applied to rules or parts of rules to generate a part of the input that is invalid.

- Apply this checklist to the syntax to identify specific mutations of the valid input, each of which employs at least one generic mutation.

- Design test cases to execute specific mutations.

For each test case, specify the following items:

- Input(s) to the component
- Generic mutation(s) used
- Syntax element(s) to which the mutation or mutations are applied
- Expected outcome of the test case

Statement Testing

ANALYSIS: Statement testing uses a model of the source code that identifies statements as either executable or non-executable.

DESIGN: We design test cases to exercise executable statements.

For each test case, specify the following items:

- Input(s) to the component
- Identification of statement(s) the test case should execute
- Outcome you expect of the test case

Branch/Decision Testing

ANALYSIS: Branch testing requires a model of the source code that identifies decisions and decision outcomes. A decision is an executable statement that may transfer control to another statement depending on the logic of the decision statement. Typical decisions are found in loops and selections. Each possible transfer of control is a decision outcome.

DESIGN: We design test cases to exercise decision outcomes.

For each test case, specify the following items:

- Input(s) to the component
- Identification of decision outcome(s) the test case should execute
- Outcome you expect from the test case

Data Flow Testing

ANALYSIS: Data flow testing uses a model of the interactions between parts of a component connected by the flow of data as well as the flow of control.

Assign categories to variable occurrences in the component, where the category identifies the definition or the use of the variable at that point.

Definitions are variable occurrences in which you give a new value to a variable. Uses are variable occurrences in which you do not give a new value to a variable. (You can further distinguish uses as either data definition P-uses or data definition C-uses. Data definition P-uses occur in the predicate portion of a decision statement, such as while ... do, if ... then ... else, etc. Data definition C-uses are all others, including variable occurrences in the right-hand side of an assignment statement, or an output statement.)

Derive the control flow model for the component and identify the location and category of variable occurrences on it.

DESIGN: We design test cases to execute control flow paths between definitions and uses of variables in the component.

For each test case, specify the following items:

- Input(s) to the component
- Locations of relevant variable definition and use pair(s)
- Control flow subpath(s) to be exercised
- Outcome you expect from the test case

Branch Condition Testing

ANALYSIS: Branch condition testing requires a model of the source code that identifies decisions and the individual Boolean operands within the decision conditions. A decision is an executable statement that may transfer control to another statement depending on the logic of the decision statement. A decision condition is a Boolean expression you evaluate to determine the outcome of a decision. We find typical decisions in loops and selections.

DESIGN: Design test cases to exercise individual Boolean operand values within decision conditions.

For each test case, specify the following items:

- Input(s) to the component
- Each decision evaluated by the test case, identification of the Boolean operand to be exercised by the test case and its value
- Outcome you expect of the test case

Branch Condition Combination Testing

ANALYSIS: Branch condition combination testing requires a model of the source code that identifies decisions and the individual Boolean operands within the decision conditions. A decision is an executable statement that may transfer control to another statement depending on the logic of the decision statement. A decision condition is a Boolean expression we evaluate to determine the outcome of a decision. We find typical decisions in loops and selections.

DESIGN: We design test cases to exercise combinations of Boolean operand values within decision conditions.

For each test case, specify the following items:

- Input(s) to the component
- For each decision evaluated by the test case, identification of the combination of Boolean operands to be exercised by the test case and their values
- Outcome you expect from the test case

Modified Condition Decision Testing

ANALYSIS: Modified condition decision testing requires a model of the source code that identifies decisions, outcomes, and the individual Boolean operands within the decision conditions. A decision is an executable statement that may transfer control to another statement depending on the logic of the decision statement. A decision condition is a Boolean expression that is evaluated to determine the outcome of a decision. We find typical decisions in loops and selections.

DESIGN: We design test cases to demonstrate that Boolean operands within a decision condition can independently affect the outcome of the decision.

For each test case, specify the following items:

- Input(s) to the component

- For each decision evaluated by the test case, identification of the combination of Boolean operands to be exercised by the test case, their values, and the outcome of the decision

- Outcome you expect from the test case

Static Analysis (aka Source Code Analysis)

Source code analysis products employ a technique called variable tracing. Developers use these tools to inject test data into the application during security testing to study the software's potential values and behaviors through the call graphs that represent data flows through the application. By injecting test data this way, the source code analysis product infers what behavior may occur for a certain scenario and variable value-some refer to this technology as an "inference engine."

The danger of the source code analysis technique is that it produces inferences, or guesses, as to how the system might behave during run-time and production configuration conditions. Source code analysis can only determine possible security vulnerabilities in the application, which usually results in high false positive rates during security testing.

In the security testing field, trusting the inferred results of source code analysis is analogous to trusting that an application will function according to design when it compiles cleanly. If all code is syntactically and semantically correct, then it will compile. But do you have confidence that it will meet the functional requirements simply because it compiled? Similarly, developers who rely on source code analysis to infer security problems in the application must also perform additional security testing to validate the application's real run-time behavior with respect to the potential vulnerabilities.

Black-Box Testing Techniques

The four most common techniques and approaches of black-box testing are described here.

Smoke Test

A subset of the black-box test is the smoke test. This test is a cursory examination of all of the basic components of a software system to ensure that they work. Typically, smoke testing is conducted immediately after a software build is made.

The term comes from electrical engineering, where in order to test electronic equipment, power is applied and the tester ensures that the product does not spark or smoke. This test ensures that future testing is not blocked.

Equivalence Partitioning

ANALYSIS: Equivalence partitioning uses a model of the component that partitions the input and output values of the component. The input and output values are derived from the specification of the component's behavior.

Each partition contains a set or range of values, chosen so that all the values can reasonably be expected to be treated by the component in the same way (that is, they may be considered equivalent). Valid and invalid values are partitioned in this way.

DESIGN: We design test cases to exercise partitions. A test case may exercise any number of partitions and the following items must be specified:

- Input(s) to the component
- Partitions exercised
- Outcome you expect from the test case

Test cases are designed to exercise partitions of valid values and invalid input values. We may also design test cases to check that invalid output values cannot be induced.

Boundary Value Analysis

ANALYSIS: Boundary value analysis uses a model of the component that partitions the input and output values of the component into a number of ordered sets with identifiable boundaries. These input and output values are derived from the specification of the component's behavior.

The model comprises bounded partitions of ordered input and output values. Each partition contains a set or range of values, chosen so we can reasonably expect all the values to be treated by the component in the same way (that is, they may be considered equivalent). Both valid and invalid values are partitioned in this way. We normally define the partition's boundaries by the values of the boundaries between partitions. However, where partitions are disjointed, we use the minimum and maximum values in the range that makes up the partition. We consider the boundaries of both valid and invalid partitions.

DESIGN: We design test cases to exercise values both on and next to the boundaries of the partitions. We produce three test cases for each identified boundary, corresponding to values on the boundary and an incremental distance on either side of it. We define this incremental distance as the smallest significant value for the data type under consideration.

For each test case, specify the following items:

- Input(s) to the component
- Partition boundaries exercised
- Outcome you expect from the test case

Test cases are designed to exercise valid boundary values and invalid input boundary values. We may also design test cases to test that invalid output boundary values cannot be induced.

User Input Validation

You must validate user input to conform to expected values. For example, if the software program is requesting input on the price of an item and is expecting a value such as 3.99, the software must check to make sure all invalid cases are handled. A user could enter the price as "-1" and achieve results contrary to the design of the program. Other examples of entries that could be entered and cause a failure in the software include: "1.20.35," "abc," "0.000001," and "999999999." These possible test scenarios should be entered for each point of user input.

Other domains, such as text input, need to restrict the length of the characters that can be entered. If a program allocates 30 characters of memory space for a name, and the user enters 50 characters, a buffer overflow condition can occur.

Typically when invalid user input occurs, the program either corrects it automatically or displays a message to the user that their input needs to be corrected before proceeding.

Dynamic Analysis (aka Black-Box Security Testing)

Also known as "automated penetration" or "fuzz testing," dynamic analysis occurs when a security tool actively attacks the running application based on thousands of known vulnerabilities and attack patterns. A dynamic analysis tool executes thousands of hack attempts on the application in a matter of minutes, just as a hacker would over days or weeks.

The danger of taking only the dynamic analysis approach is that it can be less thorough than source code analysis because it does not have access to, or detailed knowledge of, the application source code. Dynamic analysis tools are used during security testing to crawl an application like a web spider to discover all of its pages and files and then use this site map to direct automated hack attempts. If the tool is unable to "guess" where some pages or files are located, or is blocked by complex authentication or session management, then it would not be able to effectively attack and assess the security of those hidden resources. The developer can then end up with a false sense of security.

Consider the example of a cross-site scripting vulnerability whereby an attacker is able to embed malicious code into an application and trick a user into executing the code on their own machine. During security testing, a source code analysis product might be able to identify the potential of a cross-site scripting vulnerability by finding unvalidated inputs or poor session handling, if the particular language and compiler is supported. This information is useful to a developer when pinpointing potential problems. But efforts can be misdirected or wasted when developers spend time fixing a potential vulnerability that in reality is not even exploitable in the application.

Hybrid Analysis

Analysis tools, such as source code analysis or dynamic analysis, are alone only a partial solution.

To increase the reliability of security testing results, security testing should be a combination of analysis techniques, using source code analysis information to direct a second, more practical approach called dynamic analysis. This allows developers to identify vulnerabilities more accurately and confidently than with either technique individually. This combination approach, known as *hybrid analysis*, produces the accurate and reliable security information that developers need to assess the security of their code.

A hybrid analysis tool, which will know about the cross-site scripting possibility from an analysis of the source code, will target this potential vulnerability during the dynamic analysis phase of security testing. The tool can determine whether the page is exploitable by attempting to hack it. Furthermore, dynamic analysis can also identify vulnerabilities in a third-party component or database code that source code analysis would not uncover, since it doesn't have access to the third-party component's source code.

The hybrid analysis approach of HP DevInspect combines source code analysis with dynamic (black-box) testing to reduce false positives and find more security defects during development. First the source code analysis technology defines the application's attack surface and identifies all inputs that could potentially be exploited. Then, the dynamic testing phase uses the intelligence gleaned from the source code analysis to execute a series of attacks using automated hacking techniques that reduce false positives and yield the actual exploitable security vulnerabilities in the application.

HP Application Quality Management Solutions Introduction and Overview

Because this book was intended to focus more on practical process and methodologies for testing, we did not discuss the technology aspects of testing in detail. It's important to note that most of the concepts presented in this book can be implemented, digitized, or automated with HP's quality-management solutions for applications.

HP Quality Center

An integrated, web-based system for performing quality assurance across a wide range of environments, HP Quality Center contains applications that support and automate critical quality activities. These include requirements management, test management, issue tracking, and automated functional and business-process testing.

HP Quality Center is powered by an enterprise-level J2EE platform that serves as a central repository for all quality assets, houses centralized workflow rules, and facilitates collaboration among all parties involved in the quality process. The application foundation ensures 24/7 availability, scalability, performance, and redundancy of the Quality Center to make sure it's available to all users at all times, including complex, geographically distributed Centers of Excellence.

HP Quality Center consists of the following components:

HP TestDirector for Quality Center software — Includes these core modules: Release Management, Requirements Management, Risk-based Test Management, Test Plan, Test Lab, and Defect Management. These modules offer a seamless, consistent, and repeatable process for all stages of application quality management — from gathering requirements, to planning and scheduling tests, analyzing results, and managing defects and issues. All HP quality-management applications are web-based and allow data traceability across the entire application lifecycle, which means you can trace business requirements to functional requirements, defects to tests.

All the information collected during the quality process needs to be processed, aggregated, and analyzed to provide solid basis for decision-making. Rather than traditional "reports," HP Test Director for Quality Center offers an integrated dashboard, which is designed to provide an executive-level view of the entire quality process. The project manager can get a clear understanding of what's going on with the process, project, performance, and quality across multiple IT projects and initiatives, to make informed release decisions. In addition to reporting the high-level status, the integrated dashboard provides the drill-down capabilities to help determine the root-cause of a particular problem and take corrective measures.

HP QuickTest Professional software — An advanced automated testing solution for building functional and regression tests. It features a unique keyword view and active screen technology to radically simplify test creation and maintenance. HP QuickTest Professional software provides functional and regression test automation for major software applications and environments, including next-generation development technologies, such as Windows Presentation Foundation, web services, Macromedia Flex, .NET, J2EE and ERP, and CRM applications. It offers a fresh approach to automated testing by deploying keyword-driven testing, and it radically simplifies test creation and maintenance. Using keyword capabilities, testers can build test cases by capturing flows directly from the application screens and applying robust capturing technology (record/replay). In addition, power users get full access to the underlying test and object properties through an integrated scripting and debugging environment.

HP Business Process Testing software — The new way to approach test automation. Unlike the traditional record-replay tools, HP Business Process Testing involves business analysts — who know the most about application functionality and common uses — in the process of creating automated, reusable, test components. The business analyst can use familiar tools like spreadsheet grids to describe the common business process flow through the application. Using non-technical language, they can describe what's being done on each screen and what results are expected. After the business process flows have been documented, the automation engineer — who is familiar with powerful automation solutions like HP QuickTest Professional software — creates reusable test components and stores them in the HP Quality Center repository. The business analyst can then drag-and-drop those components to create complete business processes, such as order entry and customer contact management.

HP now offers an SAP-specific version of its Business Process Testing software to make it easier and more cost effective to test SAP applications. HP Business Process Testing for SAP accelerates test-flow creation and maintenance in an SAP environment. It can learn new SAP transactions in an implementation or upgrade project, and automatically break them into a set of reusable business components. It can then detect changes in the SAP application and update tests on an ongoing basis, making test execution and maintenance significantly cheaper.

HP Change Impact Testing Module for SAP Applications — Provides an automated process for identifying changes, analyzing technical impact, evaluating business risk, optimizing the test strategy, and creating a test execution plan. It helps QA teams make informed decisions as they allocate testing resources to large volumes of change requests. The granular and comprehensive coverage of changes provides impact visibility even to non-experts. As part of an integrated quality assurance solution, the software specifically highlights the areas where testing is most critical.

HP Service Test and Service Test Management software — HP's application-testing know-how extends here to address the new and complicated world of testing SOA services. HP Service Test is geared toward pure services testing with the following capabilities: decoupling (API and protocol-layer) validation, shared services functional testing, full coverage of SOA interfaces (multiple protocol support, SOAP, web services over HTTP, WS over Java Message Service, MQ). HP Service Test software reduces the need for manual testing and addresses the complexity of test management. It's fully integrated with the entire HP Quality Center solution family.

HP Performance Center Suite

HP Performance Center software — An enterprise-class performance testing platform designed to enable both global standardization and the formation of a performance testing center of excellence (COE). This solution allows performance-testing teams to standardize and centralize distributed-application performance with a single web-based solution. HP Performance Center software is powered by HP LoadRunner. It adds enterprise capabilities and features that provide a standard, centralized platform for running performance tests around the globe and around the clock.

HP LoadRunner software — The industry-standard performance testing solution; it drives load, diagnoses problems, and helps deploy application with no surprises. Using minimal hardware resources, HP LoadRunner emulates hundreds or thousands of concurrent users to apply production workloads to virtually any client platform or environment. HP LoadRunner stresses an application from end to end — applying consistent, measurable, and repeatable loads — then uses the data to identify scalability issues that would impact real users in production.

HP LoadRunner supports performance testing for a wide range of application environments and protocols, including web, SOA and web services, Ajax, RDP, database, legacy, Citrix, Java, .NET, and all major ERP and CRM applications, including PeopleSoft, Oracle, SAP, and Siebel. HP LoadRunner has more than 40 non-intrusive monitors tailored for these systems and provides diagnostics for J2EE, .NET, Siebel, Oracle, and SAP. HP LoadRunner offers one set of rules for all enterprise load testing requirements.

HP Application Security Center

These solutions enable your developers, QA teams, and security experts to successfully conduct web application security testing and remediation. This sophisticated, scalable, web application security solution helps you find and fix security vulnerabilities for web applications throughout the application development lifecycle. The Application Security solutions are fully integrated with HP Quality Center so as security vulnerabilities are identified, they are captured, managed and tracked in HP Quality Center seamlessly — like any other application defect.

HP WebInspect software — Web application security assessment software designed to thoroughly analyze complex web applications for hidden security vulnerabilities. It delivers fast scanning capabilities, broad assessment coverage, and accurate web application scanning results. HP WebInspect is designed to handle Web 2.0 complexities and is capable of identifying vulnerabilities that are undetectable by traditional scanners. The solution offers unique capabilities including simultaneous crawl and audit (SCA) and concurrent application scanning, resulting in fast and accurate, automated web application security testing.

HP QAInspect software — Allows QA professionals to incorporate fully automated web application security testing into your overall test management process without the need for specialized security knowledge and without the risk of slowing aggressive product release schedules. Tight integration with HP Quality Center allows security vulnerabilities to be treated like any other software defect.

HP DevInspect software — Simplifies security for developers by automatically finding and fixing application security defects and helping developers build web applications and web services with advanced security features quickly and easily without affecting schedules or requiring security expertise. HP DevInspect uses a hybrid analysis approach that combines source code analysis with black-box testing to reduce false positives and find more security defects.

HP Assessment Management Platform — Automates web application assessment by providing an enterprise view of application security with centralized control and risk management for your security teams. The solution offers self-service access for developers, QA professionals and line of business managers who need security information for the web applications they are developing, testing and deploying as well as the ability to find and fix application security defects. Developers, QA teams and security professionals can collaborate to remove security vulnerabilities early in the software lifecycle, reducing the risk of security breaches. Additionally, they can focus on remediation of vulnerabilities instead of how and when to perform scans.

For more information on all of the solutions listed here, please visit www.hp.com/go/btosoftware.

Appendix C

Verification

Introduction

While it is not the intention of this book to go into depth on the subject of verification, it is a very important topic. In this appendix, we will give a short overview of the process. We sometimes call this process testing without testing.

Most of the time when we say testing, we mean something like "running the thing." So, how do we test without running the thing? How do we test without "testing"?

Let's take a closer look at our definition. The purpose of testing is to finds bugs, right? So if we expand our definition to include any activity intended to find bugs, then we go beyond just running the thing. We can include reviewing in our testing definition. Execution-based testing is called *validation*, and non-execution-based testing is called *verification*.

Can we review code instead of executing it? Yes. Of course, most of our software is pretty complex, so reviewing it may not be all that efficient, but it is certainly worth a try.

Then, is reviewing code the best use of our time? That depends. It depends on where the bugs are that we're trying to find. Interestingly, industry averages tell us that 70 percent of the defects are actually in the requirements and design. So, if we can review things like requirements, specifications, designs, and the like, we can prevent possibly 70 percent or more of the defects before we even begin the "testing."

One of the problems with this, though, is that most people say, "We don't have time for all that stuff." This is a reasonable gut reaction, but the numbers don't bear this out. Actually, every time someone has tried to measure the resource and schedule impact of verification, they get the same result: **Projects are faster and cheaper if you do verification than if you don't.**

A variety of terms are in use to describe the process. Most commonly, we call this *peer review* or *technical review*. We'll use the general term, verification, in the section that follows.

Several levels of formality may be used. We'll discuss an overview of the most formal level; you can tailor this for your own needs. Consider the complexity of the work product, the risk if the final product fails, and the maturity of the organization and its tolerance for process. (There is a huge difference between process and procedures, but we won't go into that here.)

Let's look at the basics.

Verification is a process designed to identify — and thus eliminate — defects in all manner of work products. Examples of these work products include requirements, functional specifications, test plans, source code, user interface layouts, and others. The basic concept is that an ad hoc team comes together for the purpose of reviewing a work product. The author of the work product uses the review process to make sure that the product is as complete, clear, and correct as possible.

The members of the review team each play a specific assigned role. The roles are:

- **Author** — This role is self-assigned. This person is the one who created the work product in the first place.

- **Moderator** — This person has the responsibility to manage the entire review, and keep the meeting from devolving into either a design session or a free-for-all!

Not everybody wants this role, and not everybody who does want this role is suited for it.

■ **Recorder** — This person takes the notes. This should *not* be the author or moderator.

■ **Reviewers** — These are the folks who do the actual content review and present their findings.

■ **[Observer]** — This is an optional addition to the team. The observer is usually there to learn how the process works so he or she can be prepared to take an active role in the future. We usually qualify this by saying that observers must have the moderator's permission to attend. Their role is to, as the name implies, observe, and not participate.

■ **[Subject matter expert]** — This is an optional addition to the team. Sometimes it helps to have an additional member of the team who can clarify the matter at hand and may also be able to help describe what is technically feasible.

There may be some overlap among the roles. For example, the moderator and the subject matter expert may also be reviewers. Note that for the author, there is no overlap: the author cannot fill any of the other roles.

There are eight steps in the process, as follows:

1. Planning
2. Kickoff
3. Individual Review
4. Collation / Discussion Preparation
5. Discussion
6. Defect Logging
7. Revision / Confirmation
8. Final Report

The following table shows who is involved at each of the steps.

	Author	Moderator	Recorder	Reviewers
Plan	✓	✓		
Kickoff	✓	✓	✓	✓
Individual Review	(✓)	(✓)		✓
Collation	(✓)	✓		
Discussion	✓	✓	✓	✓
Defect Logging		(✓)	✓	
Revision / Confirmation	✓	(✓)		✓
Final Report	(✓)	✓		

Steps

Planning

Role	Action
Author	■ Select/request a moderator. ■ Assist moderator in his/her tasks.
Moderator	■ Assign roles. ■ Create review package. ■ Schedule meetings.

When an author determines that his or her work product is ready for review, he or she must first get someone to serve as moderator. The moderator functions as an overall coordinator of the review activities. In the planning stage, the moderator first assesses the readiness of the work product for review.

"Readiness" means there is a high likelihood of successful completion of the review. If the moderator determines that there are too many defects in the work product, for example, he or she may deem that the work product is not ready and suggest that the author clean it up before submitting the work product for verification.

Assuming readiness, the moderator selects individuals for the review team and assigns them their roles. The people chosen should represent the various stakeholders. Since almost all work products are responses to predecessor work products, one or more of the team members could be people who were responsible for the predecessor. Since almost all work products are the drivers for follow-on work, some of the team members could be people who must perform the next step or steps.

For example, consider the case of a product-requirements document. This is the response to a marketing-requirements document, and therefore one member of the review team could be the author of the marketing-requirements document. This allows for assurance that the product-requirements document correctly interprets the marketing requirements. Similarly, the product-requirements document is input to the functional design description and the test plan, so team members could include both the person who will create the functional design description and the person who will create the test plan.

Generally, one should avoid having as a team member any manager who has his or her own employees on the review team. It is occasionally necessary to ignore this rule, but one should do so with caution. Some people are less comfortable in this situation than others.

The ideal size for the review team is five to nine people.

The review package consists of the work product, any predecessor documents, and the standard for the type of article. The package may be hard copy, soft copy, or merely pointers to where the information exists.

Kickoff

Role	Action
Moderator	■ Distribute review package. ■ Conduct meeting. ■ Secure commitments.
Author	■ Present high-level overview of the items to be reviewed.
Reviewers	■ Listen and learn. ■ Ask questions.
Recorder	■ Log duration of the meeting. ■ Log list of attendees.

At the kickoff meeting, the team gets information about the work product. If the review package is hard copy, it is distributed at this meeting. Because the team may be scattered across several locations, the material must be available for all team members at this time.

The kickoff meeting is intended to be quite brief. It generally lasts no more than 30 minutes. At the meeting, the author will give a brief summary of the article, and may alert the team to areas of concern. It may also happen that some areas of the article are not completed, and so the author would point this out. Those areas may be subject for review at a later date.

The kickoff should be at least five working days prior to the discussion for the reviewers to have sufficient time for their individual review. This allows the reviewers the flexibility to weave their preparation around their primary assignments. As an alternative, the team may decide how long they need and schedule the discussion as a result of that decision at the kickoff.

If any reviewers feel that they cannot complete the individual review in the allotted time, this is their opportunity to either opt for replacement or suggest a different date for the discussion.

The moderator should remind the team members of the purpose of the technical review. The purpose is to develop findings for the work product, not to redesign the article.

The recorder's function here is to log the number of attendees and the duration of the meeting. This information will be useful later when we are calculating the return on investment (ROI) of the process.

Note that the kickoff meeting does not necessarily need to be a face-to-face gathering. In fact, it may be that team members are in different locations. Consider conference calls and video hook-ups. In some circumstances, email might also be considered as an alternative. There are some disadvantages to this, but it may occasionally be necessary.

Individual Review

Role	Action
Reviewers	■ Review the article. ■ Record findings. ■ Transmit findings to the moderator before the discussion.
Moderator	■ Monitor reviewers' progress. ■ Help reviewers with process issues.
Author	■ Answer questions from the reviewers.

During this step, the reviewers perform their individual review and gather their findings. The findings belong in one of the following categories:

- ■ defects
- ■ questions

- external issues
- praise

Using discrete categories helps assure that the review does not devolve into a redesign exercise. The category list may be upgraded or modified from time to time, but not on a product-by-product basis. This will allow for project comparisons and statistical analyses.

Defects

The defects fall into one of five types:

- **Error** — A statement is incorrect.

- **Conflict** — A statement is in disagreement with a different statement in the work product.

- **Missing** — Some necessary or required information is not present.

- **Extra** — Some feature or design has been added that is not accounted for in the predecessor document. For example, if there is no requirement for a particular product to run on some platform, then having a specification or design to support that platform would be a defect of type "extra."

- **Unclear** — A statement in the work product has several possible interpretations or is written in a way that could confuse the user of the article.

It should be noted that the defects identified during Individual Review are not recorded in the Incident Management database at this time. That action occurs after the discussion, after consensus has been reached that the finding is, in fact, a defect.

Questions

Some findings are questions to be asked of either the author or subject matter expert. Generally, these are requests for background information or information that is nominally outside the area of the work product. One word of caution: if a reviewer has a question, it may be that something is missing or unclear. Either of these situations would be a defect, not a question.

External Issues

Sometimes, reviewers uncover difficulties that are relevant to the use of the product being developed, but not under the control of the team doing the developing. For example, if a specification calls for use of a third-party application, a potential external issue could concern run-time licenses for that application.

Praise

It is useful to take note of things that are done especially well in the work product, so that others may learn. Besides, many authors feel a bit sensitive about having their work scrutinized, and it's nice to complement them. Of course, the goal is to conduct the reviews in such a way that no one feels picked on, but as the process is introduced, there may be a bit of trepidation.

The reviewers transmit their findings to the moderator the day before the discussion. Any errors such as typos, grammatical errors, spelling errors, and the like should be sent separately from the findings. These will be handed over to the author and not covered in the meeting. (Some people just like to use marked-up copies of the article for this purpose.)

Collation

Role	Action
Moderator	■ Gather findings. ■ Prepare agenda.
Author	■ Assist moderator.

The moderator collects the findings and prepares the agenda for the meeting. Most moderators choose to handle the findings in page sequence rather than skipping all around in the work product. Occasionally, there may be reasons for placing a particularly serious problem first regardless of its location.

If many defects are being reported, the moderator should consider canceling the review, since the work product may not be quite ready. In this situation, the findings should be given to the author for use in updating the article. A review can then be rescheduled.

Discussion

Role	Action
Moderator	■ Keep discussion focused on identification, not solution. ■ Keep discussion focused on the work product, not the author.
Reviewers	■ Present findings. ■ Participate in determining review result.
Recorder	■ Log prep time for each reviewer. ■ Finalize the findings log. ■ Summarize findings at end of discussion. ■ Log duration and attendees.
Author	■ Listen and learn. ■ Answer questions if asked. ■ Thank the reviewers for their help.
Observer	■ Observe.
Manager	■ Stay away.

A suggested agenda is:

- ■ Moderator distributes copies of agenda and collation report to reviewers.

- Moderator describes purpose of meeting, process, and ground rules.

- Moderator polls reviewers, asking how much time they spent in their preparation. If any of the reviewers are not prepared, they should change role from reviewer to observer if they wish to remain. If too many reviewers are not prepared, the meeting should be rescheduled for another time.

- Moderator polls reviewers for any general comments before beginning a point-by-point review. This may include general praise or comments about missing items that cannot be pegged to a particular location in the work product.

- Each of the identified findings is presented in sequence. If any of the findings is a question, the team decides if this indicates a defect or not. If it is not a defect, the author answers the question. For findings of type defect, consensus is reached on the severity and type.

- Group searches for new defects. These would be findings not previously reported. Typically, the earlier discussion may trigger observations in the team that no one individual had reported.

- Recorder notes any new findings as well as changes to the previously identified findings. This includes the description, severity, and type. The severities are:

  1. The end product would be unusable if this were not fixed.

  2. A major function of the end product would be unusable if this were not fixed.

  3. A feature (part of a function) of the end product would be unusable if this were not fixed.

  4. A particular situation would cause a failure in the end product if this were not fixed.

5. This would not necessarily result in an observable failure in the end product, but could potentially cause some difficulty or annoyance.

■ Recorder reads the list of findings. This gives the person who reported it a chance to add clarification if necessary, and gives the author a chance to ask any final questions about it. It also gives the team a chance to hear the entire list, which is useful if forming an overall impression. This helps with the determination of the discussion outcome.

■ Team determines the outcome. Four possible outcomes are:

- **Accept as is** — No changes are necessary.

- **Accept with changes** — Author makes the changes based on the findings. No confirmation is necessary.

- **Revise with informal confirmation** — Author makes changes based on the findings. The changes are informally confirmed.

- **Revise and hold another formal review** — The findings are significant enough that the team decides that another formal review is needed after the author has made the changes.

■ If the outcome was "Revise with informal confirmation," the team decides on the confirmation technique(s), as well as assigning individuals to the confirmation as appropriate. Examples of informal confirmation techniques are:

- One person from the review team confirms (no meeting).

- Several people from the team confirm (no meeting).

- Author presents changes to team (meeting).

■ Author collects any marked packages that may contain the typos, etc., if they have not been previously transmitted.

- Author thanks the team members.

The discussion should last no more than two hours. It is sometimes necessary to divide an article into sections to achieve this goal. Rarely, an article is long, complex, and cannot be divided. In this case, the meeting may have to exceed the two-hour limit.

Defect Logging

Role	Action
Recorder	■ Log defects to the incident management database.

Following the discussion, the recorder enters the defects into the incident management system. This is not the onerous chore it may seem to be, for two reasons. First, because most of the defects will have been transmitted electronically, cut-and-paste can be used. Second, the expectation is that the number of defects found will not be prohibitive, or the discussion would not have taken place. As an alternative, some review teams may choose to use a less formal method of tracking the defects, such as a spreadsheet. (On the other hand, if you are going to copy the information to a spreadsheet, why not just go ahead and copy it to the incident manager so you can take advantage of the tools available?)

Revision, Confirmation

Role	Action
Author	■ Revise the work product as indicated by the review findings.
Moderator	■ Monitor revision progress. ■ Assure all revisions have been made.
Reviewers	■ Confirm revisions as assigned during the discussion.

Final Report

Role	Action
Moderator	■ Summarize the verification. ■ Perform statistical analysis as needed. ■ Make recommendations as appropriate.

The statistical analysis addresses issues such as number of findings of each type and how much time on average was spent per finding.

Appendix D

Naming Conventions

Numbering of Test Cases

T0–T100	Positive test cases that result in processing of data
T200–T299	Positive test cases that result in processing of data and are based on a test rule that contains a combination
T900–T999	Test cases that lead to a error message

Numbering of Expected Results

R1–T100	Positive results
R200–R299	Positive result of a combination
R900–R999	Error message

References

Chapter 1

Ohno, Taiichi. *The Toyota Production System.* ISBN 0-915299-14-3.

Standish Group International, Inc. *CHAOS Report.*

National Institute of Science and Technology (NIST). 2002 study.

Boehm, B. and V. Basili. "Software Defect Reduction Top 10 List," *IEEE Computer.* IEEE Computer Society. Vol. 34, No. 1, January 2001, pp. 135-137.

Chapter 2

United States National Institute of Standards and Technology.

Fagan, Michael. www.mfagan.com.

NASA. *Software Formal Inspections Guidebook.* NASA-GB-A302.

Robertson, James and Suzanne Robertson. *Mastering the Requirements Process.* Addison-Wesley Professional, 1999.

Chapter 4

Princeton Softech, an IBM company.

Chapter 5

Juran, J.M. *Quality Control Handbook*. McGraw-Hill, 1988.

Giga Information Group 2001. "Justifying IT Investments: Quality Assurance."

Chapter 7

Open Web Application Security Project (OWASP). http://www.owasp.org/index.php/Top_10_2007.

Wagner, Ray, et. al. "Recommendations for Security Administration, 2006." Gartner. Feb 13, 2006.

Sutton, Michael, Jeremiah Grossman, Sergey Gordeychik, and Mandeep Khera. "Web Application Security Statistics." Web Application Security Consortium. http://www.webappsec.org/projects/statistics.

Sources for the illustration, page 156: "Rise in application attacks," Computer Emergency Response Team Coordination Center (CERT/CC), National Vulnerability Database, Open-Source Vulnerability Database, Symantec Vulnerability Database.

"2007 CSI Computer Crime and Security Survey." Computer Security Institute. http://www.gocsi.com/forms/csi_survey.jhtml.

"2007 Annual Study: U.S. Cost of a Data Breach." Ponemon Institute. http://www.vontu.com/uploadedfiles/global/Ponemon-Cost-of-a-Data-Breach-2007.pdf.

Gartenberg, Marc. "How to develop an enterprise security policy." Computerworld. http://www.computerworld.com/securitytopics/security/story/0,10801,98896,00.html.

Benson, Christopher. "Microsoft Best Practices for Enterprise Security: Security Strategies." Microsoft TechNet. http://www.microsoft.com/technet/archive/security/bestprac/bpent/sec1/secstrat.mspx?mfr=true.

Gartenberg, Marc. "How to develop an enterprise security policy." Computerworld. http://www.computerworld.com/securitytopics/security/story/0,10801,98896,00.html.

Allen, Julia. "Governing for Enterprise Security." Carnegie Mellon University, Software Engineering Institute. http://www.cert.org/archive/pdf/05tn023.pdf.

Meier, J.D., Alex Mackman, and Blaine Wastell. "Threat Modeling Web Applications: What is Threat Modeling." Microsoft Developer Network. http://msdn2.microsoft.com/en-us/library/ms978516.aspx#tmwa_whatisthreatmodeling.

"Threat Model." Wikipedia. http://en.wikipedia.org/wiki/Threat_model.

Meier, J.D., Alex Mackman, and Blaine Wastell. "Threat Modeling Web Applications. Microsoft Developer Network. http://msdn2.microsoft.com/en-us/library/ms978516.aspx.

Howard, Michael. "Mitigate Security Risks by Minimizing the Code You Expose to Untrusted Users." Microsoft Developer Network. http://msdn2.microsoft.com/en-us/magazine/cc163882.aspx.

Scambray, Joel, Mike Shema, and Caleb Sima. *Hacking Exposed Web Applications*, 2nd Ed., page 430. McGraw-Hill Osborne Media, 2006.

Chapter 8

Dun & Bradstreet, Barometer of Global Outsourcing.

Womack, James P., Daniel T. Jones, and Daniel Roos. *The Machine that Changed the World*, ISBN-13 978-0060974176.

International Software Testing Qualifications Board (ISTQB). http://www.istqb.org/download.htm.

Chapter 9

Six Sigma, Motorola, Inc.

About the Authors

Andreas Golze is practice director within C&I at Hewlett Packard, driving the global practice for Application Lifecycle Optimization. He helped develop the HP Software Quality Model, now the standard for many large-scale enterprise organizations around the globe. Andreas has more than 20 years' experience in the IT industry. Before his move to HP, he was senior executive of the TestLab at SQS AG, responsible for developing and expanding partner business. Andreas studied computer science and business at the University of the Armed Forces in Munich. He began his career as a NATO programming officer in Belgium.

Mark Sarbiewski, senior director of product marketing, joined Mercury Interactive (now HP Software) in 2003. Mark oversees the design and implementation of HP's product marketing and go-to-market activities for Applications within the BTO portfolio. Mark was VP of marketing for InterTrust Technologies. He was a principal consultant for five years with Pittiglio, Rabin, Todd & McGrath, the leading management consultant firm for technology companies. Mark also spent four years with IBM, where he was an application software engineer. He received his B.S. in computer science and mathematics from University of California at Davis, and earned his MBA from University of Virginia's Darden Graduate School of Business.

Alain Zahm joined Hewlett Packard in 2007 as principal for the Application Lifecycle service practice for Europe, the Middle East, and Africa. With 20 years' experience in the IT industry, Alain has worked in software and telecom product development, and with large systems-integration projects. As VP for risk management in Atos Origin's global service line, he was responsible for operational issues of enterprise integration projects and risk evaluation for large bids. As Schlumberger-Sema's director of innovations for global consulting and systems integration, Alain focused on innovation and business development. He studied software engineering at the Paris VI University and the Ecole Nationale Supérieure des Mines de Saint-Etienne, where he earned both a Masters and a PhD.

Glossary

abstraction	1. The level of technical detail of some representation of software.
	2. A cohesive model of data or an algorithmic procedure.
acceptance criteria	The exit criteria that a component or system must satisfy to be accepted by a user, customer, or other authorized entity.
account	A group of projects belonging to a single customer, practice, or technology.
analysis	Set of activities that attempts to understand and model customer needs and constraints.

audit	An independent evaluation of software products or processes to ascertain compliance to standards, guidelines, specifications, and/or procedures based on objective criteria. An audit includes documents that specify: ■ The form or content of the products to be produced. ■ The process by which the products will be produced. ■ How compliance to standards or guidelines will be measured.
baseline	A point at which some deliverable produced during the software engineering process is put under formal change control.
best practice	A superior method or innovative practice that contributes to the improved performance of a project under a given context, usually recognized as "best" by other peer projects.
black-box testing	Testing that does not focus on the internal details of the program but uses external requirements: ■ Functional testing ■ Regression testing ■ Pre-UAT/UAT testing ■ Load, stress, scalability and volume testing ■ Compatibility testing ■ Usability testing ■ Security and operational readiness testing
boundary value analysis	A black-box testing method that designs test cases to exercise data boundaries.

bug	A flaw in a component or system. For example, an incorrect statement or data definition, that can cause the component or system to fail to perform its required function. A bug, if encountered during execution, may cause a failure of the component or system.
business risks	A set of potential business problems or occurrences that may cause the project to fail.
business function test	The first black-box test where the functionality of each business function is tested against the requirements.
business process test	The black-box test where end-to-end business processes inside the application are tested with a focus on correct implementation of interfaces between the business functions.
certification	The process of confirming that a component, system, or person complies with its specified requirements.
change request (CR)	A document that provides detail on the type of change that is needed.
coding	The generation of source code.
compliance	The capability of the software product to adhere to standards, conventions, or regulations in laws and similar prescriptions.
complexity	A quantitative measure of a program's complexity.
component	The smallest software item that can be tested in isolation.

concurrency testing	Testing to determine how the occurrence of two or more activities within the same interval of time, achieved either by interleaving the activities or by simultaneous execution, is handled by the component or system.
configuration	The collection of programs, documents, and data that must be controlled when changes are to be made.
configuration management (CM)	A discipline applying technical and administrative direction and monitoring to: ■ Identify and document the functional and physical characteristics of a configuration item. ■ Control changes to those characteristics. ■ Record and report change processing and implementation status. ■ Verify compliance with specified requirements (IEEE Std. 610.1990).
coverage	The degree, expressed as a percentage, to which a specified coverage item has been exercised by a test suite.
customer	The person or group that has requested the application or software and will be paying for its development.
CMMI	Capability Maturity Model Integrated — A model developed by Software Engineering Institute (SEI) of Carnegie Mellon University (CMU) to sort out the problems relating to the use of multiple Capability Maturity Models.
design	An activity that translates the requirements model into the next level of granularity, to facilitate software development.

defect	A flaw in a component or system that can cause the component or system to fail to perform its required function. For example, an incorrect statement or data definition. A defect, if encountered during execution, may cause a failure of the component or system.
defect management	The process of recognizing, investigating, taking action on, and disposing of defects. It involves recording defects, classifying them, and identifying their impact.
documentation	Descriptive information.
efficiency	The capability of the software product to provide appropriate performance, relative to the amount of resources used under stated conditions.
effort	The work-time product (for example, person-days) associated with a project.
equivalence partitioning	A black-box testing method in which the input domain of a program is divided into classes of data from which test cases can be derived.
errors	A lack of conformance found before software is delivered to the customer. In HPGM-AS, the terms "error" and "defect" are used interchangeably.
estimation	A project-planning activity that attempts to estimate effort and cost for a software project.
enterprise resource planning (ERP)	A business management system that integrates all facets of the business, including planning, manufacturing, sales, and marketing.

exit criteria	The set of generic and specific conditions, agreed upon with stakeholders, for permitting a process to be officially completed. The purpose of exit criteria is to prevent a task from being considered complete when there are still outstanding parts of the task that have not been finished. Exit criteria are used by a testing team to report against, and to plan when to stop testing.
formal review	A review characterized by documented procedures and requirements. For example, inspection.
functional requirement	A requirement that specifies a function that a component or system must perform.
functional testing	Testing based on an analysis of the specification for the functionality of a component or system. See also black-box testing.
goal	Goals are broad, general intentions that are abstract and intangible.
go/no-go decision	A point at which manager or the customer decides whether the project should proceed.
hardware (H/W)	Refers to physical objects that can be touched, like disks, disk drives, display screens, keyboards, printers, boards, and chips; in contrast, software cannot be physically touched.
high-level test case	A test case without concrete (implementation level) values for input data and expected results.
impact analysis	The assessment of change to the layers of development documentation, test documentation, and components to implement a given change to specified requirements.

informal review	A review not based on a formal (documented) procedure.
integration testing	Testing performed to expose defects in the interfaces and in the interactions between integrated components or systems.
interface testing	An integration test type concerned with testing the interfaces between components or systems.
ISTQB glossary	The definitions of most of the terminologies specific to software testing was produced by the Glossary Working Party of the International Software Testing Qualifications Board. For more information, see http://www.istqb.org/downloads/glossary-current.pdf.
ITIL glossary	The official ITIL glossary (for IT Service Management - ITSM) is available here: http://www.get-best-practice.co.uk/glossary.aspx?product=ictinfrastructurelibrary
keyword-driven testing	A scripting technique that uses data files to contain not only test data and expected results, but also keywords related to the application being tested. The keywords are interpreted by special supporting scripts called by the control script for the test.
lifecycle	A linear, sequential approach to process modeling. A partitioning of the life of a product into phases that guide the project from identifying customer needs through product retirement.

load test	A test type concerned with measuring the behavior of a component or system with increasing load. For example, the number of parallel users and/or numbers of transactions determines what load can be handled by the component or system.
maintainability	The degree to which a program is amenable to change.
maintenance	The activities associated with changes to software after it has been delivered to end-users.
metrics	Quantitative measures of the process or the product.
milestones	A point in time used to indicate progress during a project.
modularity	An attribute of a design that leads to the creation of high-quality program components.
object-oriented	An approach to software development that makes use of a classification approach and packages data and processing together.
objectives	Goals are broken down to a set of well-defined objectives, with the intention that achievement of the narrow, precise, tangible, and concrete objectives will translate to achieving the goal. Objectives in turn get broken down to tasks and activities.
outsourcing	Contracting software work to a third party.
operational readiness test	A final phase of testing performed on the prospective production system after all other cutover activities are complete, prior to going live into production.

portability	A characteristic attributed to a computer program if it can be used on operating systems other than the one in which it was created without requiring major rework. Porting is the task of doing any work necessary to make the computer program run in the new environment.
productivity	Work output per unit time.
project plan (PP)	A description of the management approach for a project containing a detailed plan of major project phases, milestones, activities, tasks, and the resources allocated to each task.
project planning	The activity that creates the project plan.
project risks	The set of potential project problems or occurrences that may cause the project to fail.
performance test	Testing that is conducted to determine the performance under a real-world workload. The test may measure throughput, volume limits, transaction time, etc.
precondition	Environmental and stated conditions that must be fulfilled before the component or system can be executed with a particular test or test procedure.
priority	The level of (business) importance assigned to an item, for example, high, medium, low.
peer review (PR)	Review of work products performed by peers during development of the work products to identify defects for removal.

quality	1. The degree to which a product conforms to both explicit and implicit requirements.
	2. The ability of a set of inherent characteristics of a product, product component, or process to fulfill requirements of customers.
quality assurance (QA)	A series of activities that assist an organization in producing high quality software; a planned and systematic means for assuring management that defined standards, practices, procedures, and methods of the process are applied.
regression testing	Tests that are conducted repeatedly to ensure that a change has not introduced side effects.
reliability testing	The process of testing to determine the reliability of a software product.
resources	Anything that is required to execute a project: people, hardware, materials, information, etc.
re-testing	Testing that runs test cases that failed during a previous test, to verify the success of corrective actions.
review	An evaluation of a product or project status to ascertain discrepancies from planned results and to recommend improvements. Examples include management review, informal review, technical review, inspection, and walkthrough.
risk	A risk is an uncertain event or condition that, if it occurs, has a positive or negative effect on a project objective. A risk has a cause and, if it occurs, a consequence.

risk analysis	The process of assessing identified risks to estimate their impact and probability of occurrence (likelihood).
risk-based testing	Testing oriented towards exploring and providing information about product risks.
risk management (RM)	An organized, analytic process to identify what might cause harm or loss (identify risks), assess and quantify the identified risks, and to develop and, implement (if needed) an appropriate approach to prevent or handle risk causes that could result in significant harm or loss.
root cause analysis (RCA)	A structured, team-based, analytical approach that when used correctly can alleviate chronic failure problems in a product or application.
requirements management (RM)	The management of all requirements received by or generated by the project, including both technical and non-technical requirements, as well as those requirements levied on the project by the organization.
requirements verification	The phase in the HP Quality Methodology where by the end user adds acceptance criteria to each business requirement, thus validating the completeness and correctness of the requirements, ensuring traceability to business functions and ensuring testability.
return on investment (ROI)	The ratio of revenue from output (product) to production costs that determines whether an organization benefits from performing an action to produce something.
scalability	The capability of the software product to be upgraded to accommodate increased loads.
scalability testing	Testing to determine the scalability of the software product.

security testing	Testing to determine the security of the software product.
severity	The degree of impact that a defect has on the development or operation of a component or system.
scope	Scope is a boundary statement that indicates the sum of the products and services that must be provided as a part of the project.
software engineering	A discipline that encompasses the process associated with software development, the methods used to analyze, design and test computer software, the management techniques associated with the control and monitoring of software projects, and the tools used to support process, methods, and techniques.
smoke test	A subset of all defined or planned test cases that cover the main functionality of a component or system, to ascertaining that the most crucial functions of a program work, but not bothering with finer details. A daily build and smoke test is among industry best practices.
stress testing	Testing conducted to evaluate a system or component at or beyond the limits of its specified requirements.
stub	A skeletal or special-purpose implementation of a software component, used to develop or test a component that calls or is otherwise dependent on it. It replaces a called component.
software (S/W)	Computer programs that tells a computer's hardware what to do.
software build	Either the process of converting source code files into executable code or the result of doing so.

software development lifecycle (SDLC)	The software development lifecycle is a general model of the software development process in which the life of the product is partitioned into phases (stages), which guide the project team from customer needs identification through product retirement.
SEI	The Software Engineering Institute is a federally funded research and development center sponsored by the U.S. Department of Defense through the Office of the Under Secretary of Defense for Acquisition, Technology, and Logistics (OUSD [AT&L]).
service level agreement (SLA)	A contract between a service provider and a customer that specifies the services the project will furnish. SLAs may often include the percentage of time services will be available, number of users that can be served simultaneously, and help-desk response time.
SME	A subject matter expert is an individual who is an expert in an area of specialization.
stakeholder	Individuals and organizations that are actively involved in the project, or whose interests may be positively or negatively affected as a result of project execution or project completion; they may also exert influence over the project and its results.
system test	Testing that is conducted on the complete integrated system to evaluate the system's compliance with its specified business requirements.
syntax testing	A black-box test design technique in which test cases are designed based upon the definition of the input domain and/or output domain.

technical reviews	A structured meeting conducted by software engineers with the intent of uncovering errors in the deliverable or work product.
test automation	The use of software to perform or support test activities, for example, test management, test design, test execution, and result checking.
test approach	The implementation of the test strategy for a specific project. It typically includes the decisions made based on the (test) project's goal and the risk assessment, starting points regarding the test process, the test design techniques to be applied, exit criteria, and test types to be performed.
test cases	The creation of scenarios and data that can be used to uncover errors in the software.
test coverage	The degree, expressed as a percentage, to which a specified coverage item has been exercised by a test suite.
test environment	An environment containing hardware, simulators, software tools, and other support elements needed to conduct a test.
test requirements	The requirements for the system under test, which are derived from the business requirement or business functions. The test requirements are a common reference for business analysts and IT.
test plan	A document that describes the objectives, scope, approach, and focus of a software testing effort. The process of preparing a test plan is a useful way to think through the effort needed to validate the acceptability of a software product.

test summary report	A document summarizing testing activities and test results. It also contains an evaluation of the corresponding test items against exit criteria.
testing	Testing involves operation of a system or application under controlled conditions and evaluating the results. The controlled conditions should include both normal and abnormal conditions. Testing should intentionally attempt to make things go wrong to determine if things happen when they shouldn't, or things don't happen when they should. It is oriented to "detection."
tools	Application software used to perform software engineering tasks. For example, design tools, testing tools.
traceability	The ability to identify related items in documentation and software, such as requirements with associated tests.
unit testing (UT)	Testing of individual hardware or software units or groups of related units.
user	The individual who actually uses the software or product that has software embedded within it.
user acceptance testing (UAT)	Formal testing conducted by users or their representatives on a new or changed information system, to enable a user, customer, or other authorized entity to determine whether to accept a product or product component.
validation	Confirmation by examination and through objective evidence that the requirements for a specific intended use or application have been fulfilled.

variable	An element of storage in a computer that is accessible to a software program by referring to it by a name.
verification	Confirmation by examination and through the provision of objective evidence that specified requirements have been fulfilled.
white-box testing	A test case design technique that makes use of the knowledge of the internal program logic, for example, unit testing.

.